Boys in Schools

This book is to be returned on
or before the date stamped below

UNIVERSITY OF PLYMOUTH

EXMOUTH LIBRARY

Tel: (01395) 255331
This book is subject to recall if required by another reader
Books may be renewed by phone
CHARGES WILL BE MADE FOR OVERDUE BOOKS

Boys in Schools

Addressing the real issues –
behaviour, values and relationships

Editors, Rollo Browne and Richard Fletcher

FINCH PUBLISHING
SYDNEY

Boys in Schools: Addressing the real issues – behaviour, values and relationships

First published by Finch Publishing,
PO Box 120, Lane Cove, 2066, Australia.

98 5 4 3

Copyright © Rollo Browne, Richard Fletcher and Finch Publishing, 1995.

National Library of Australia
Cataloguing-in-Publication entry:

Boys in Schools

Bibliography
ISBN 0 646 23958 9 ✓

1. Boys – Education – Australia. 2. Boys – Australia – Psychology.
3. Sex role in children – Australia. 4. Social interaction in children – Australia. 5. Educational psychology – Australia. I. Browne, Rollo.
II. Fletcher, Richard, 1947– .

371.821

Photographs by David Hancock.
Cover and text design by Steve Miller/Snapper Graphics.
Typeset by DOCUPRO, Sydney.
Printed by Brown Prior Anderson, Burwood, Victoria.

Publisher's note

Photographs   The photographs by David Hancock on the pages of this book have been included to illustrate everyday moments in the lives of boys in schools. The people featured in these photographs are in no way connected with the individual stories, characters or situations presented in this book. We are grateful to David Hancock for representing so imaginatively the lives of young people and to the schools concerned for their permission to reproduce these photographs.

Further information   The 'Notes' section of this book contains references to various chapters and further information on specific points mentioned in the text. Contact addresses for the contributors are provided for readers who wish to request additional details about specific programs.

Contents

Foreword

When I was in school, especially high school, there were only two ways to succeed as a boy – sport or study. All boys felt themselves to be ranked on one of these two pyramids of success – a few at the top, and the great mass of us squashed beneath.

Being a sports type or 'jock' had short-term glory, but usually didn't lead anywhere, career-wise. Our school's swimming hero spent his twenties in prison for involvement with hard drugs. On the other hand, academic excellence was also a lonely path. The leading 'nerd' of my year committed suicide shortly after learning that he had not scored perfectly in the HSC. So you could excuse me for thinking that (for boys) success could be something of a health hazard. Perhaps the problem was that it was all too unbalanced. There weren't enough different ways to be a boy.

High school in the Sixties wasn't all bad, though. Many parts of my secondary schooling were wonderful. There was much warmth and resilient humour amongst the boys (though we never talked about our lives or our feelings) as well as tentative (but still affirming) contacts with girls.

There were also some great teachers – great in all different kinds of ways. These men and women took us on amazing journeys into new aspects of being a boy – and of being human. In bushwalking, yoga, poetry, film studies, English, camps and excursions, we not only glimpsed a larger world, but began stepping into it – beyond our parents' suburban dreams (or perhaps not – who knows of what they dreamed?). The Duke of Edinburgh's Award was introduced at our school during the backlash against cadets and led to all kinds of broadening experiences. It enabled us to get to know teachers in smaller groups and out of classroom settings. There was nothing airy-fairy about what we were learning. Through our teachers, we learnt the truth about the Vietnam holocaust, into which, one way or another, we were soon to be swept.

As adults we tend to forget how central teachers' personalities are in kids' lives. Their kindness, humour, strength – or the lack of these – make or break a child's school day. At our school we certainly had the full range – psychopaths and losers, as well as women and men who had gotten their lives together, and who had something quite precious to give to struggling youngsters. Many years later, when I saw the movie *Dead Poets' Society*, it didn't seem to me to be at all unrealistic – I knew teachers like that.

Lately I have seen the insides of lots of schools. My work has changed from being a psychotherapist to an activist – working to change and 'liberate' men from the narrow role that industrial society has given them. This includes the world of boys. I've been invited to schools at every level and in every corner of Australia to talk about the psychology of boys.

Many schools today (rich and poor) are emotional, if not physical, jungles. Each day, underresourced and overworked teachers (often in bleak surroundings and striving to fulfil impossible expectations) 'do battle' with children who have been wounded by parental failure and family breakdowns. I have visited schools where everyone is scared all the time, from the principal down. The need for structure, safety and respect – as described by Fred Carosi and other contributors in these pages – is a prerequisite for any kind of basic learning, let alone personal growth. And (as David Shores asks in his chapter, 'Boys and Relationships') how can teachers help kids unless we meet their needs too?

The goal of building admirable men has traditionally been a claim made by schools, but rarely addressed in a concrete way. Now this is starting to change. Wider society is becoming aware, too, and wants schools to respond. Richard Fletcher's riveting statistics on boys' lives, in 'Changing the Lives of Boys', will jolt everyone who reads them. His other chapter, 'Looking to Fathers', is also a most important call to involve fathers in schools.

In schools around Australia there has always been a lot of good 'boyswork', though not by that name. But we need more, and it has to be more conscious. We have to counter the signals sent to boys (from society, the media, from some women who hate men, and some men who hate themselves) that being male is somehow intrinsically dirty, dangerous and inferior. Many boys now get this rejected feeling from all sides: overstretched or neglectful parents, stressed-out teachers, the lingerie ads, soft-porn rock videos and from girls (who, with their social powers and verbal skills, have an ability to wound – even unintentionally).

We have to make the world of boys – the playground and classroom – safer and freer of ridicule, shaming and sheer physical danger. Readers of my book, *Manhood*, may recall the story of a five-year-old boy on his first day at school, who talked too much and was told by the teacher to go and stand by the rubbish bin. He misheard, and stood in the bin. The teacher did not correct him, and he stayed there till the bell. This is hardly a subtle message.

Several obstacles can get in the way of doing good work with boys. The first is to think that 'boyswork' consists solely of conducting groups in schools, trying to get boys to be better behaved towards girls and women. This approach is well intentioned but counterproductive. Nobody ever changes at a deep level as a result of coercion, pressure or blame, however gently phrased or cleverly worded. Kids know when they are being 'got'. They will react with ridicule or say the 'right' things to get you off their backs.

Boys will change when they are helped to understand themselves better, are affirmed and valued 'as they are' and are given the tools to feel safe and equal around girls. They will only listen to teachers who listen to them without preaching. Boys do respond to discipline and to being confronted but only by people who show them respect and who care about them. Rollo Browne, in these pages, points out the need to work from the inner experiences of boys and to not impose on them in a moralising way.

Men who work with boys need to meet several criteria. They have to be at ease with their own masculinity (including its lusts, angers and energies) and to have arrived at a safe place through resolution not social compliance. And those men and women who would teach boys have to have a genuine liking, in fact a love, of boys – with their scruffiness, noisiness, in-your-face honesty and surprising capacity for tenderness and vulnerability. Maureen Moran's short, shining chapter, 'Young and Powerful', should be read by every teacher, principal and parent in the country. Maureen Moran and Annie McWilliam have been successful with very rough boys and, here, share their experiences. Their positivity about the intrinsic worth and goodness of every boy is an inspiration.

Another big danger in boys' education is the oversimplification posed in the 'buzzword' term, 'Social Construction of Gender'. This is probably a wonderful and enlightening theory. I cannot say, as I have always fallen asleep at lectures on the subject. (Most mysterious

– as I am usually an alert person.) The problem with 'Social Construction theory' lies in what people take it to mean. That is, that gender is purely socially shaped, starting with a blank slate. Put another way: that boys and girls are born identical and then we make them different – and if we could just make them the same, then everything would be fine.

The fact is, not only do boys and girls differ hormonally, in thinking styles, in developmental rates and so on, but these differences intensify at certain ages, especially the mid-teens. The situation is confused even more by the fact that individuals differ too, so that some girls are more biochemically 'masculine' than some boys, and some boys more biochemically 'feminine' than most girls. And so we have to look at individual differences too.

If we don't accept and deal with the fact of this, then we are being cruel and unusual in our treatment of real live human beings, at a vulnerable time in their lives.

Here is just one instance of a biological difference having a bearing in the classroom. Many boys are six months behind girls in fine-motor development when they enter Year 1. This is a real physical difference. They actually need far more movement and activity than a seat at a desk affords, and are much less able to handle pens, scissors and other mechanisms. So they are immediately disadvantaged. For some, their careers as problem learners are set in motion.

It's time we honoured and put a positive value on the unique qualities of boys. Pre-industrial societies recognised that there is a high-energy creativity in boys' make-up which must be channelled well and understood, and certainly not ignored. The fact that we even address boys' needs at all has provoked talk of a backlash from some quarters. But we must move beyond this and avoid a competitive frame of reference. We must redouble our efforts to liberate women and girls, and also start changing the male of the species – or all gains will be lost.

To conclude, the need for this kind of book is urgent. The writings collected here are early beginnings – diaries from the coalface. They are tentative forays into the big questions about masculinity. If reading this book makes you think about your ways of working with young people, then the contributors and editors will have done their jobs. We are well started on the road to creating happy boyhoods and a more rounded, positive masculinity.

Steve Biddulph, Coffs Harbour, Winter 1995.

Introduction

We started on this book because it was obvious

to us that, as a group, boys are in trouble.

Not every boy, not the same kind of trouble and

not all of the time – but enough of them across

all ethnic and socio-economic groups to know

there is a pattern.

Trouble at school, in
the streets, at home.
Boys putting others
downs constantly.
Put-downs as a way
of relating to others.
Boys doing crazy, risky
things in order to belong to a group, to go one step better.
Boys getting one-up on each other, scoring points, acting out.
Boys treating girls as stupid, as only good for sex.
Boys harassing anyone who is different.
Boys bullying, threatening violence, carrying weapons.
Boys as 'innocent' onlookers, urging others to fight.
Boys turning against learning in school – 'It's cool to be a fool'.
Boys struggling with how to 'be' in the world – how to be power-
ful, how to succeed.
Boys getting abused, humiliated and saying nothing.
Boys growing into men.

Traditionally the response has been, 'Well, boys will be boys'. This is cold comfort to those parents and teachers living and working with these boys day by day.

Much has been written about parenting. More recently there has been an emphasis on raising boys. The role of fathers is being recognised as increasingly significant. While parenting skills and understandings in this area are important, we believe that no matter how well a parent has raised a son, this is not the sole, determining influence on the child. As the child grows older, spending less time with family and more time with peers, the parents' influence shrinks. The world of the young person becomes more focused on peers, movies, television and the interactions within social groups.

It is in schools that children first spend substantial time away from their homes. School playgrounds and classrooms are places where children get together in large numbers and interact. It is here that boys and girls divide themselves into, and are treated as, distinct groups. Boys, as well as girls, form and create links based on language, clothing, size, interests, sports, rough-and-tumble – almost anything at all.

These groups allow individuals to belong. By their very nature such groups include some and exclude others. Certain behaviours are encouraged; other behaviours are shunned. It is apparent that boys often form groups based on ridicule and competition. For some, fitting into the peer group is more important than learning. This is easier to see at high schools but is no less present at primary schools.

Schools are significant shaping grounds for both young men and women. In particular, schools are faced day by day with having to manage large numbers of students and their problematic behaviours – bullying, harassment and put-downs, attention seeking, failure to complete work, disruptive behaviour and so on. In the majority of cases this means controlling the boys. How this is done sets one of the tones of the school.

What can schools do about it? What do parents want schools to do about it? What influence do schools really have in the way masculinity is shaped?

The many contributors to this book have tried, through their different perspectives, to build a picture of work going on in schools related to gender and masculinity. It is an area that touches the desires of parents and educators to create a better world for our children. How we do this and what we mean by it are vital issues. We are, after all, talking about people's lives and relationships. What parents do about it, what schools do about it, can be hotly argued. Our view is that all positions have a place in this debate.

Rollo Browne, Sydney, July 1995

there are many voices in this book. Some come from frontline workers with boys. Classroom teachers working within the existing curriculum and school structures have noticed boys' dilemmas and have tried, within the constraints of their schools, to do something different. The chapters on teaching History by Alan Littlewood, English by Wayne Martino, Drama by Kathy Kokoris and Media Studies by Su Langker, give first-hand accounts of some of the pioneering work being done in Australian classrooms. It is not accidental that these examples come from the humanities.

It is in the nontechnical subjects that boys have done most poorly compared with girls. This is not a reflection of boys' natural abilities (or disabilities) but a result of the cultural values and attitudes which surround 'scientific' versus 'expressive' subjects. In the future, the way we teach physics and mathematics and engineering to boys will also come under challenge. The values built into the teaching style, content and evaluation of all subjects, not just those of the humanities will come to be redesigned for better educational and life outcomes for boys.

On another level are the whole-school approaches to boys' issues. The attempt to interest senior high school boys in all school activities reported by Peter Ireland, has a focus on the benefits overlooked by boys in their staying uninvolved. Maria Pallotta-Chiarolli's work addresses boys' involvement in a homophobic school culture. The account by Fred Carosi and Ross Tindale of the concerted program to address violence at Canterbury Boys High School includes another important feature. The use of approaches which may be directed at boys' problems in this instance, but which may also be adopted by the school for other reasons. Boys can benefit from approaches and programs which may not be just for boys.

A third view comes from those working across schools. Peter Clarke, an antiviolence educator, developed and trialled a program using small groups of primary school boys to improve relationships skills and cooperative behaviour. David Shores, while working as a behaviour-support teacher two days a week, injected into the Boys and Relationships program (described in his chapter) some of his knowledge and skill gained from working with men in domestic violence programs. Gwenda Sanderson has many years of experience in a particular education setting – after-school classes for students (mostly boys) with reading difficulties. She uses this concentrated training to suggest practical strategies for involving boys in reading. Bullying is one issue which involves both girls and boys, but there is enough difference, in frequency, style and outcome to warrant particular attention to boys. Basing her chapter on her work as a psychologist with many schools, Coosje Griffiths provides a blueprint for effective action in this area.

I have two relevant roles: as a father visiting schools to run Stopping Rape workshops for boys; and as a health researcher briefing school staff on the health implications of boys' education. I have drawn on my experience as a high school science teacher to offer a broad view of the possible role of fathers in schools.

As one of the few male family-planning educators in NSW, Rollo Browne has honed his boy-management skills while teaching sexuality and personal development in high schools. His chapter, 'Working with boys and masculinity', offers a practical approach to dealing with concepts underlying almost any approach to boys' work. 'Schools and the construction of masculinity', his final chapter, provides a means to bring a wide range of activities into a coherent approach to educating boys.

For anyone who has had some contact with boys' issues in schools, this list may appear unfinished. Special groups, such as Aboriginal, migrant or disabled boys, stand out as deserving thoughtful attention. Sport, personal development and other key subjects require further consideration, and many issues (for example, the benefits of segregated classes) remain unresolved.

Many of the chapters do acknowledge the newness of their approach. This means that the evalution of programs and other initiatives targeting boys and masculinity should be a priority for schools. However the airing of evidence on what is being done in the name of boys' education in Australia is timely. Not only because State and Federal governments are moving to build boys' concerns into the various policy documents, but because across Australia there is a recognition that simply noticing that boys are faring poorly, in education, in health, in relationships, is not enough. It is time to identify promising moves at all levels which address these issues in a way that values boys without glamorising their destructive behaviours.

This book is our attempt to foster a positive, thoughtful shift in educating boys to make a better society for all our children.

Richard Fletcher, Newcastle, July 1995

Cowering
behind the
bushes

Bullying and teasing can ruin the school lives of students and create shattering after-effects. *Coosje Griffiths*, an experienced teacher, psychologist and national consultant on bullying issues based in Perth, Western Australia, describes the characteristics of bullying and reports on how a whole-school program can work.

Chad's story

In response to a magazine article on bullying, I received a phone call from a father who was very distressed. The father said that his son, Chad, had been suffering from bullying. He had approached the school for help on numerous occasions.

The main perpetrator of the bullying was verbally able and popular. The school had a mixed and uncoordinated response to this problem. Staff responses over a period of time included punitive measures towards the perpetrator, such as detention and verbal warnings regarding possible suspension. The response by the staff involved tended to put the onus on Chad to make changes, including moving to an new class and receiving counselling at the school and by a psychiatrist.

The school measures aimed at dealing with the problem resulted in more subtle attacks and 'underground' bullying involving psychological games. The school had difficulty in viewing the bullying as a problem because of the lack of external evidence – no physical forms of bullying could be proven.

Chad's situation was worsened by the fact that he was not living at home.

Chad suicided at the age of seventeen soon after leaving school. The note he left behind cited that bullying was the cause of the suicide, particularly the actions of one boy. Subsequent reports on the suicide pointed to a lack of 'duty of care' on the part of the school.

The need for a whole-school approach

In the UK, and also recently in Japan, it has taken national media attention on the issue of suicides resulting from bullying to activate the education and justice authorities into developing national strategies. Norway was the first country to recognise the devastating effects of bullying as a result of three suicides related to bullying being reported in one year. National student surveys, research and whole-school strategies were developed as a result.

The tragedy is that schools often have a fragmented approach to bullying incidents. This leads to punitive measures towards the victims and/or the bullies that rarely bring about long-term change. A whole-school approach has been found to be the best basis for real change in the attitudes and practices of students, teachers and parents.

Effective intervention often involves more than one strategy. Working out the first step is usually the hardest. There are four targets of intervention:

- the child;
- the family;
- the school; and
- the wider community.

Sometimes simple strategies with the child or the school may produce positive results. In other cases, it may be necessary to have a combined effort at a number of levels over a long period of time.

Shame and peer culture

Bullied boys will suffer enormous shame about being bullied, especially as they enter the teenage years. Often the very aspects of themselves about which they feel most sensitive are the targets of the bullies. Teenage boys are particularly sensitive to taunts about their sexuality, especially about a physical feature that can't be changed or being thought of as 'poofter' or 'gay'.

The peer culture rejects the options of the victim getting help or 'dobbing' (either by the witnesses or the victim). To make things worse, staff will even reinforce the notion that the victims should be able to stand up for themselves, a common saying being, 'Don't be such a wimp'.

Adolescence is also a time when boys want to become independent of adult help. Consequently, in that climate, few boys are likely to seek help from adults. Surveys in Western Australia support the findings in other countries which show that up to forty-five percent of boys indicate that they have been bullied in the last three months. Only a small percentage of these children, as few as five percent, ask for help. Even when they do tell, they are often reluctant to allow any action to be taken.

What makes it bullying?

Confusion between bullying and the healthy 'rough-and-tumble' activity of boys (or fights involving boys of relatively equal strength), has resulted in unhelpful responses to bullying. Typically we hear, ' Bullying is part of growing up'; 'Bullying makes the man'; and 'People who get bullied usually ask for it'.

Bullying is a deliberate act of undermining another individual for the benefit of those involved. Boys are more likely to do it for power, status, reputation and group control – and, in some cases, for immediate material gain. At other times they may be motivated by jealousy, revenge or even boredom. It is quite common to find that a boy who has been victimised over time will, himself, adopt bullying behaviour. One former student (now a teacher) explained that his activities as a bully began when he went to a new school. He was pressured into bullying a certain individual by a group of boys whose group he wanted to join. He felt he had no option, as he was in fear of the threat of group exclusion and possible victimisation if he did not comply.

The characteristics of bullying

Bullying is characterised by the following features:

- It is a repetitive attack which causes distress at the time as well as further distress resulting from fear of the threat of future attacks.
- It is characterised by an imbalance of power.
- Its nature may be:
  - verbal (e.g., humiliating put-downs)
  - physical (e.g., hit, kick, punch, poke with objects)
  - social (e.g., rumours, ignored, ostracised)
  - psychological (e.g., threatened by staring, stalking, 'dakking', taking personal possessions, notes, blackmail, etc.)
- Bullying can be defined by measuring the effects that the acts have on the vulnerable child.
- The basis of bullying is an attitude rather than an act.

The nature and dynamics of bullying – and the fact that it is often hard to detect – have led to it being classified as a form of abuse. The victimised boy is chosen because of his inability to defend himself, either because of the nature of the bullying or through sheer numbers.

A whole-school response

Mark, a fourteen year old, sat in my office. His hands trembled. He twisted and turned in his seat, and his eyes were downcast. He had difficulty in describing what had happened to him. (A teacher had referred him to me because he'd run out of her class crying. She had described to me how he was sitting at the end of the row and had been pushed, elbowed and verbally taunted by a number of boys in the class.

I was able to develop trust and confidence between us, and then began to explore how long this had been going on and how many students were involved. He described how it had started at the beginning of secondary school and involved boys from two different groups – one group was his social network in which he was on the periphery and the other boys were from the 'popular' group. The bullying had affected his concentration in class, and his grades had gone down. Stress-related illness had caused him to be absent from school. He had occasionally resorted to truanting as a way of handling the situation.

His typical response to my suggestions that I might work with the students who were bullying him was, 'Don't talk to them . . . things will only get worse. They'll think I dobbed.'

Mark's main form of retaliation was verbal, which the bullies later cited as their reason for harassing him in the first place. Mark was a bit behind in growth and muscular development and had a poor posture. Fortunately for Mark, he was an able student with supportive parents and some specialised sporting skills.

Strategies

Occasionally I can work with the student on their own and get results. Usually it requires developing a number of strategies at the same time. Owing to the long-term nature of the bullying, I worked with Mark at a number of levels.

Student level

After outlining how I'd talk to the bullies in a nonpunitive way, Mark was able to trust me to work with the students involved in the bullying.

We also explored his belief system, self-esteem issues and self-protective behaviours. We practised using breathing and centring techniques. We also anticipated certain social situations and ways in which he could deal with verbal taunts.

Peer level

I worked with the bullying students using the method of 'shared concern', usually referred to as the Pikas method. This is an approach which involves interviewing 'suspected' bullying students individually, which effectively takes them out of their peer-group context. The bullies were asked to comment in a general way about the negative things happening to Mark. They became involved in a problem-solving approach in which they developed a 'shared concern' about Mark in the process, and offered ways they could help him.

Staff level

Staff were informed that strategies had been put into place. The school had already been involved in a workshop at which staff learnt about different responses to incidents of bullying. Using role-plays, they shared the change in attitude experienced by the 'suspected' bullies (using the Pikas method) compared with the negative responses of suspected bullies using the traditional punitive methods. Teachers practised the Pikas method using a simple script. Two key staff members had already had a few successes with the Pikas method and so reinforced the effectiveness of the method to the rest of the staff. As it happened, the school was also in the process of putting a whole-school bullying policy into place.

Parents and community

Mark's teachers and parents were made aware of the situation and were asked to support Mark by being extra-observant and subtly offering extra positive reinforcement and attention to Mark to boost his self-confidence. It was explained that strategies to handle the situation using a problem-solving approach had been put into place. Mark's year coordinator also talked to Mark about alternative lunchtime activities and offered support.

Initially, Mark's parents wanted the bullies to be punished but realised that they preferred the situation to be changed for their son rather than to simply gain retribution.

They organised for Mark to attend a self-esteem camp to help him gain confidence. Also they realised that they needed to review their parenting and so attended a parenting workshop.

Outcomes

After a week, I interviewed the former bullies as a group to assess their progress. I then saw Mark again and noted that there had been a number of positive changes. An important achievement was a meeting between Mark and the group, which ensured that further work on problem-solving could occur. In this meeting we explored the concept of tolerance.

Three months later, Mark reported that the bullying had stopped and that there had only been occasional, minor altercations. His work standards had improved, and his parents reported that he was much easier to get on with at home. They especially noted that he was kinder to his younger brother.

Provocative victims

In contrast to Mark's case, there are boys who actively provoke bullying. Work with these 'provocative victims', poses a more difficult task. Provocative victims often have few friends and can be unpopular with teachers as well as students. It is estimated that about half of the victimised students may be of this type.

Similar strategies are used, but the victims often need more intensive, long-term work, with an emphasis on group work, social skills and family counselling.

Provocative victims display inadequate social skills to varying degrees such as being overly bossy, calling people names, showing off and not sticking to the rules in games. Their goals are to be included in groups, to make friends and to gain attention. The behaviour stems from a sense of inadequacy, low self-esteem and, in some cases, poor family relationships. For boys it often involves neglect or rejection from the father. For example, the father remarries and does not keep up contact with the son. It must also be noted that, after a period of victimisation, any boy can end up appearing to display inadequate or inappropriate social skills caused by the stress and trauma of being bullied.

Provocative victims receive little sympathy or support from students and staff alike. A common response to their plight is, 'You asked for it'. However there is no evidence that these boys have a masochistic need to be brutalised. No-one enjoys being bullied.

Success requires a great deal of patience and a more long-term commitment. Strategies usually involve individual and family counselling and social-skills training in a peer group context.

John, a provocative victim, was too frightened to attend school because of bullying. The shared-concern method with the boys concerned worked for a while, but problems resurfaced on an intermittent basis.

Over a period of two years, a variety of strategies were employed: individual and family counselling, parent participation in a parent course, inclusion in a self-esteem group, self-protective behaviours' seminars and fostering of links to particular students and staff.

Although the problems were not completely alleviated, John developed a small group of friends, a specialist hobby and became involved in a local community group. Teachers reported that he was more confident and settled in class and was less provoking (or being provoked) in class.

Bullies

Bullies are generally believed to be deprived at home, have poor academic skills and suffer from low self-esteem. Their behaviour is thought to give them a sense of power unachievable in other areas of their life.

Although some boys who bully do fit this description, a larger and more powerful group are those who have an overestimation of their own ability, display high energy levels, manage academically and manipulate others into colluding with the bullying.

They bully to gain power and peer reputation. They often appear to gain favour with their peers and teachers and keep their bullying behaviour well hidden from adult view. Closer questioning of their peers reveals that they may appear to be popular, but are not well liked.

Teachers report that they have experienced threatening behaviour from parents of some bullies and a collusion by parents with their boy's behaviour. Responses include, 'They were just defending themselves', or, 'The school is picking on them'.

Effective approaches within a whole-school policy include a clear statement about the unacceptability of bullying and its consequences. However a key to changing the bullying behaviour is to involve them in the solutions and to rechannel their leadership skills into peer programs such as peer support, mediation or counselling.

Changing a culture

Schools which are effectively bringing about long-term change are able to modify the bullying culture at all levels – with parents, students and teachers.

In order to change negative student-subcultures, they have to become involved in the process of changing the way these three groups think. Schools need to become 'telling' or 'talking' schools, where students learn the difference between 'dobbing' and asking for help to deal with unacceptable behaviours.

A key element of changing a bullying culture involves changing the responses of 'bystanders' or 'onlookers'. Most bullying incidents occur out of adult view, so the student bystander is a powerful agent of change. Through role-play and drama, students can learn effective ways of responding to and supporting the bullied student. They can be encouraged to do so.

Staff can also learn effective 'bystander' behaviours. First, they need to become aware of their part in either modelling bullying behaviour or colluding with it.

> *Feedback from surveys indicates that students believe as few as twenty-five percent of teachers deal effectively with bullying incidents in the classroom. One student commented: 'One boy called me a "wog" in a loud voice and told me to go back to my own country. The teacher said and did nothing!' (Our 'bystander' behaviours help staff respond carefully to situations such as this.)*

Awareness-raising for the whole school community is done through workshops, role-play, videos, pamphlets (distributed to the whole school community), posters and drama.

Specialist courses often become an integral part of the school program. Students who are vulnerable can be included in self-esteem groups; aggressive students can benefit from anger-management groups. A Western Australian program called 'Changing Tracks' which uses a cognitive-behaviour therapy approach, has been found effective for both groups.

Schools need to refine their programs each year. Systems using peers have been very effective once the whole-school policies and practices are put into place. These include; peer-support programs, peer counselling, peer mediation and peer-resolution systems. These programs usually involve 'former' bullies to channel their leadership skills and energies into positive directions.

Putting it together

Ultimately, bullying in schools is a safety issue. High levels of bullying result in higher levels of violence, and students who feel unsafe and unsupported at school.

In all schools, children need to know that they have a right to feel safe and that they can seek support from adults. The Protective Behaviours basic philosophy reinforces these concepts with the mottos:

- We all have the right to feel safe at all times.
- Nothing is so awful that we can't talk with someone about it.

A whole-school approach that involves the students, parents and community is essential for real and long-term change.

The following guidelines indicate the essential components for developing a systematic whole-school approach to reducing bullying.

A whole-school approach to bullying

Awareness-raising
- Recognise that bullying exists in the school.
- Define what bullying is and establish that it's not OK.
- Advertise the fact that the school wishes to reduce bullying and involve the support of administrators.

Involvement
- Involve a committee to plan and implement a program.
- Offer workshops for staff, parents and students.

Policy development
- Identify the amount of bullying that is occurring in the school: when, where, who and what (e.g., by using surveys).
- Develop a whole-school policy involving staff, students and parents.

Strategies
- Provide a range of strategies across the school system and curriculum.
- Focus on behaviour change rather than punitive action.
- Involve students in the solutions as much as possible.
- Focus on what the school wants when there is no bullying.
- Staff are to model this behaviour.
- Advertise and maintain the program through a variety of means.

Review
- Evaluate student outcomes and modify the program annually.

Parents initiating change

When Mary rang me one Sunday afternoon to describe the situation with her son, I at first thought that her case was close to hopeless.

She described the problems with her son being bullied in an all-male school which had a reputation for a bullying ethos. The attitude of the school was virtually, 'If you can't take a bit of bullying, then maybe you don't belong here'. The family had long, traditional connections to this school, and her husband (an 'old boy') did not want to consider a change.

What Mary wanted was not only to solve the bullying problem for her thirteen-year-old son, Patrick, but to also change the school's entrenched approach to bullying.

After talking through all the options in Patrick's case we decided to approach the problem from a number of angles.

Mary decided that she would bring the matter to the school counsellor. She was also planning to talk to other parents from his class whom she knew were also concerned about the problem. Then, she wanted a group of parents to pass on these concerns at a P&C meeting. Mary decided to invite students home so she could observe the dynamics between the boys. She also planned to attend the next sports day where she would be able to broach her concerns carefully with other parents.

Mary asked for flyers for my next workshops and intended to leave them with the school counsellor as well as a magazine article on the topic.

A few staff attended these workshops and a group of parents came to the parent course. After the school administrators were given copies of the handouts they decided to have an in-house workshop for selected staff who were in administration and pastoral care.

This produced important results: a whole-staff workshop and the development of a whole-school policy and action plan, including ways to monitor and review its effectiveness. The school surveyed the student population to gain insights into the extent and type of problems at the school.

This process was accelerated by media attention at the time on a separate bullying case in which the parents wanted to sue a school for neglecting its duty of care.

The school's response could have been defensive. However, with the policy well underway, the administration took the opportunity to offer a pro-active approach.

Parents approaching the school

The first thing that parents need to realise if they approach teachers and administrators about a bullying problem, is that the response may be defensive.

Often the defensive response relates to a lack of knowledge or the absence of a systematic, whole-school approach.

Parents have offered the following suggestions:

- Initially, approach the class teacher or year coordinator.
- Your first approach is extremely important.
- You need to focus on the distress of the victim, not the fault of others.
- Approaching a sympathetic staff member is sometimes helpful.
- If the incident involves assault or abuse, it should be taken seriously – and the principal needs to be contacted immediately.

When parents approach staff members, the use of conflict-resolution skills (such as those involving 'I' statements) can greatly reduce possible defensive reactions. In one case the parents carefully formulated their request on paper and practised what they would ask for before meeting the principal. This generated positive results.

> *I feel very concerned about James because I think he is being picked on by other students. This is causing him a lot of distress and he's very reluctant to come to school. I actually took him to the doctor last week because he was suffering from headaches and stomach-aches. I was told that it may be related to the stress of this situation. I've tried to help by inviting children home. However, it appears that one boy in particular keeps picking on him. He seems to be doing it behind teachers' backs. I really need your help with this. Could you make some suggestions?*

It is important to establish a time to meet again with the teacher and review how the strategies are working. If the bullying does not decrease, it may be important to enlist the help of the principal.

The principal may want to involve the school counsellor to assist with a program. As a last resort, it may be necessary for parents to contact the district office or the head office. In some cases of violence, parents may have to involve the police.

If all else fails, it is sometimes recommended that the child transfer to another class or school. However, this strategy will usually only be effective if the child has been involved in some counselling, group work or other self-esteem-building activities.

A parent seeks action

At one of my parents' courses on bullying, Peter and Carol revealed that they had been trying for months to get something done at school for their eight-year-old son, Jason.

Jason was being picked on while going to and from school, and at break-times, by an older boy from a family known for its aggressive behaviour. Jason had become so upset that he was refusing to go to school. He was having nightmares, had lost his appetite and was often complaining of headaches and stomach-aches. The family doctor said the symptoms were stress-related. The conclusion was that the bullying was the cause.

Peter and Carol continued to raise the issue of bullying through the P&C and gave the staff articles from my parents' course on bullying.

Peter described how at one point the bully had dragged Jason out from behind the bushes and physically attacked him. The principal's response was, 'Well, what do you expect if he's cowering behind the bushes?'

Peter was incensed. He felt a return of the sense of powerlessness which he himself had experienced when bullied as a child. 'I wanted to catch the bully and attack him. I wanted to do in my adult body what I couldn't do for myself as a child.'

Peter advised the principal that his only remaining option was to contact the police to ensure the physical safety of his child. The principal changed his mind and dealt with the situation.

Responses for parents

How should a parent respond to the bullying of their child? Depending on the parents' own experience of bullying, they may either overreact and become angry or brush off the seriousness of the situation. A balanced problem-solving approach is required. Also, parents need to call on all their resources – friends, family, other parents and trusted teachers – to develop insight into their child's situation and the best approach to the problem.

Many parents have involved a variety of professionals and agencies in the community. One boy was assessed by a psychiatrist who found that his problems were stress-related caused by bullying at school. The psychiatrist subsequently mediated on behalf of the parents for the school to take action.

Some parents have taken a hard look at their family dynamics and parenting practices. The child may be vulnerable in the family context, and parents may need to strengthen their child's support systems and increase the number of positive messages they give.

Techniques for the victim

The following techniques have been used successfully by a number of parents and teachers with bullied boys to assist them in regaining confidence. They are to be used in conjunction with school strategies to change the bullying behaviour.

How to deal with hurtful comments
- Use self-talk. Repeat to yourself a silent message that you can learn such as, 'That's their problem, not mine', or 'I'm OK'. Think about other positive things you enjoy.
- Imagine that an invisible shield or warm light is surrounding you, and bouncing the words off.
- Stay focused on a place or person ahead of you. Walk with purpose whilst ignoring taunts.
- Look the bully in the eye and say, 'I don't like that . . . I want you to stop' and then walk away if they persist.

Conclusions

A body of knowledge has been built up now in the area of bullying. If people act without knowledge of this, they tend to use unsuccessful approaches and often exacerbate problems.

Focus and research on bullying is relatively new in Australian schools. Traditions in many single-sex male schools have upheld bullying practices as part of the school culture, making it difficult to achieve change. On the whole, school staff have been ready and willing to make changes but have not had access to the necessary information and training.

My work in the area of bullying has included both boys and girls. Not surprisingly, there appears to be a strong cultural bias suggesting that boys need to 'tough out' bullying episodes and that it's part of the growing-up process. Such a culture – reinforced at school and home which suggests that physical and mental cruelty to children is acceptable – needs close examination.

The negative effects of bullying on young people have been grossly underestimated in the school, family and community. There are detrimental long-term effects on our society as the bullies are more than likely to remain on a continuum of misuse of power. They are more likely to be involved in domestic violence and other criminal activities. One study showed that they were four times more likely to end up with a criminal record.

Individual parents and teachers have been remarkably successful in bringing about greater awareness of bullying and changes in school attitudes to the issue. Consequently, the guidelines in this chapter are the result of many parents' and teachers' experiences – and will, I hope, assist you in dealing with a difficult and complex problem.

Bullying checklist: signs and symptoms of the effects of bullying

The following checklist offers a number of signs and symptoms to look for in a bullied child.

Emotional
- personality changes
- mood swings: angry or tearful outbursts
- disturbed sleep (bed-wetting in the case of younger children)
- signs of depression and low self-esteem
- psychosomatic complaints: headaches, stomach-aches

Physical
- nervous tics and cowed body-language
- overeating or undereating
- self-harm
- signs of bruising, cuts and torn clothing

Social
- withdrawal from family and friends
- reluctance to join in social activities

Behavioural
- truancy
- school-reluctance
- misbehaviour in class
- change in routines to and from school

Home
- bullying or taunting of siblings
- withdrawn or aggressive behaviour towards parents
- requests for extra money and the 'losing' of valuable things

Academic
- decline in work output and school grades

Coosje Griffiths, a teacher and registered psychologist, began her work in bullying in 1988 when a class which had bullying problems was referred to her. In recent years she has worked both as a school psychologist in the Education Department of Western Australia and as a national consultant on bullying issues. Coosje (pronounced Cosha) was awarded a Churchill Fellowship in 1994 and completed overseas study in the areas of bullying and harassment.

Give me
a helmet

Prior to 1988, Canterbury Boys High School in Sydney was characterised by a hostile atmosphere which worked to undermine the learning environment. *Fred Carosi*, Leading Teacher, and *Ross Tindale*, Head Teacher Welfare, describe how an approach which harnessed the commitment of the students, staff and parents overturned the existing school culture and set new and positive directions for the school.

Two police officers chased a student down the corridor as he hurled abuse at them. The policemen caught the student, threw him against a wall and handcuffed him.

A large crowd of students and teachers had gathered in the corridor and the fear and confusion in all of us was obvious. The police 'escorted' the student to their 'paddy wagon'.

One day a student came to school drunk. His best friend, a young man with 'muscles on his muscles', was concerned about his state and tried to persuade him to go home. He was rewarded for his concern with a right cross to the jaw. A vicious fight then ensued which ended with both students requiring medical attention.

Playground violence at Canterbury Boys High School prior to 1988 was dramatic and frequent. On average, the school would experience at least one serious fight at recess and two or more during the lunch break. The amount of violence seemed to be directly proportional to the length of the break. The violence that occurred was not always directed towards other students – teachers were prime targets on many occasions. In one case, a female Science teacher was confronted while on playground duty by a group of boys, one of whom produced a knife. On another occasion, another Science teacher intervened in a playground incident and asked the student to accompany him to the deputy principal's office. The student walked behind the teacher and 'king hit' him.

Violence – an everyday occurrence

The students' behaviour in the playground was a serious problem. A regular activity was fruit fights. Students would bring oranges, lemons, tomatoes etc. to school and gangs of students would pelt each other with the fruit. One student almost lost the sight of an eye after being hit with a lemon.

Interesting responses to the situation were observed in the behaviour of the staff. In one instance, a History teacher donned a motor cycle helmet before going out to playground duty. He was afraid, quite seriously, of being hit and refused to step outside without protection.

Sometimes the violence was not so overt. A 'pack' mentality existed amongst the students. Groups of them – eight or ten in number – would sidle up to staff members and intimidate them by their physical proximity. Female members of staff were constantly targeted by the students for this type of treatment. The anonymity of being in a large group made it possible for students to get away with making offensive remarks which humiliated and intimidated many teachers.

Vandalism was rife. Both the school's and teachers' property were targeted. Teachers' cars were favourite objects of attention: they were set on fire, had windows smashed, were broken into, scratched, written on and, of course, had badges removed. Some examples of vandalism displayed creativity by students. One teacher had his car's exhaust pipe stuffed with nails, scrap metal and potatoes . . . the explosion was impressive.

Violence and intimidation were not the sole provinces of the student body at the school. While corporal punishment was phased out in 1986, a number of teachers still used bullying tactics to intimidate and/or humiliate students they did not like or who were in trouble for some reason. Such actions by staff did little to establish good relationships or set appropriate examples for students.

Classroom behaviour

Problems in the classroom were also very obvious. The noise that came from some classrooms was deafening! Both teachers and students shouted at one another. Students refused to go to classes. When questioned as to why, the answer most often given was, 'Because I don't feel like it!'.

Learning for many was, at best, a low priority. The problem was that although the majority of students wanted to learn, some teachers were not allowed to teach. On one occasion, I noticed a teacher in tears, she had just come out of her classroom. The students had refused to cooperate and she could not go on with the lesson. These sorts of classroom situations were destroying staff morale.

Teachers coped with disruptive students in a variety of ways. A popular method was to phone the offending students' parents. One particular parent complained to the school after receiving seven phone calls from seven different teachers in one day! Another strategy was to put students on 'Conduct Cards'. This almost worked when students were on the cards, but as tools for behavioural change they were useless. One teacher who was having problems, proclaimed to a class, 'If you don't like my classroom rules you can leave and see the head teacher!'. All the students left the room . . . discipline problem solved.

Teacher stress

Staff absenteeism and the willingness of casuals to work at a school are always key indicators of how positive the climate (teaching and learning conditions) of a school is. Prior to 1988, the poor health of the teaching staff was nothing short of abysmal. On a good day there would be four or five staff out of forty-five away, on a normal day it would be around eight to ten. On many occasions, casual staff specifically requested not to be called by our school again. One casual teacher worked at the school for only twenty minutes before walking off the premises in disgust.

'I want to learn'

However, these anecdotes – disturbing and amusing – present only a skewed view of the situation. There were also some good things happening in the school and some excellent teaching and learning was taking place. Most importantly, the majority of students were friendly and wanted to learn. They, too, were showing signs of frustration at the lack of structure that existed within the school. One student took matters into his own hands. During one of his classes a disruptive student was making it impossible for the lesson to continue. He got out of his seat, walked to the back of the room and punched the offending student in the face shouting, 'I am here to get an education!' before calmly resuming his seat.

A student survey was conducted in 1986 which gave a clear indication of students' attitudes towards disruptive behaviour:

- Seventy percent of students believed that disruptive students were not adequately dealt with.
- Eighty percent of those surveyed believed that this disruptive behaviour made it difficult to learn.
- Only thirty percent believed that the school's discipline system worked.

Something must be done

Staff were also surveyed, and it became obvious that they were also very unhappy with the situation. Staff identified problems such as poor staff–student relationships, vandalism, aggressive behaviour, disruptive behaviour and a lack of structure in the discipline system. If this negative cycle of disruptions and poor relationships was allowed to continue, the school would face closure. Student numbers were rapidly declining and the school's image in the community was causing concern. So 1986 was the 'crunch' year for Canterbury Boys High School. Something had to be done . . . But what?

The cry went up around the school: 'We have rules . . . people just aren't using them!'. After a dusty copy of the school rules was unearthed, it was discovered that these people were right. A group of stalwarts was charged with the task of revamping the rules. This was done with some speed, since the situation was critical. The seriousness was highlighted by the fact that a staff meeting was held after school for the rules to be discussed, amended and approved.

Each proposed rule was put to the meeting in the form of a motion and debated in a formal manner. It was impressed upon all present that by voting for a particular rule they were making a commitment to that rule from which deviation would be a heresy and punishable by derision from your peers and a half hour with the principal discussing your future career prospects. The meeting went well. There was a sense of achievement and a belief that 'something had at last been done'.

By the middle of 1986, the euphoria had evaporated and nothing had changed! Why? The experience had taught us several things. Firstly, there is no such thing as a 'quick fix'. People are slow to abandon things that don't work and it seems that we owe it to the past to 'give it one more try'. Secondly, a new structure must be developed from scratch. Thirdly, and most importantly, the new structures had to be built with the help and participation of the students and parents. Negotiation became the focus.

Start again

In early 1986, a welfare committee had been formed to find out what students, staff and parents believed to be the major discipline problems and how these problems could be addressed. The Welfare Team's findings would form the basis for developing a new system. These findings were presented at an after-school conference. This was a very important exercise because it gave all groups a chance to express their concerns. Furthermore, it provided a forum for investigating alternative systems. It also emphasised that this procedure was consultative and was to involve the whole school community. In August 1986, the conference was held, attended by staff, students and parents. The data gathered was discussed in small groups. Lectures by guest speakers focussed on 'alternative methods of discipline' and the final session was devoted to 'future directions'.

The Welfare Team's surveys showed some interesting trends (it is beyond the scope of this paper to go into details).
- Seventy-five percent of students surveyed found the existing system to be inconsistent and unfair.
- Seventy-five percent said that the school should run courses which improved self-discipline.
- Eighty percent believed that a fair way to resolve problems was for students to work it out with their class teacher, yet eighty-three percent reported that they had never done this.

The staff survey showed that their concerns centred around lack of student cooperation, aggressive behaviour, rudeness, noise and vandalism, all of which were having a negative effect on the learning environment and causing teacher stress.

In general, parents felt that discipline should be more strict and they wanted to be informed 'early' if their sons were heading for trouble.

The conference decided to proceed with a Glasser-style system which would reflect the needs of the students at Canterbury Boys High School. The Glasser method of managing student behaviour is based upon the principle that students must learn to be responsible for their own behaviour and use negotiation as a means to achieving this end.

An action plan was to be developed by the Welfare Team with the aim of having a new system in operation by the start of the 1988 school year. A year to develop a system may seem like a long time, but because so many groups needed to be consulted every step of the way and the fact that we were starting from scratch meant that this was a reasonable timetable to follow. In the meantime, it was decided to hold a residential in-service on self-esteem for staff.

Action

The self-esteem conference was held at Leura in March 1987. Its aim was to make staff more aware of the importance of self-esteem in the learning process. It also looked at strategies for raising both student and staff self-esteem on a whole-school basis. The conference was a crucial step in building the foundations of our new welfare/discipline system. It developed group cohesion, promoted negotiation, enhanced understanding of some student behaviours, was a 'concrete step' (i.e. something was happening), and most important, it provided a philosophical basis for a discipline system.

The Welfare Team developed the Action Plan with set goals and a timeline for implementation. Staff were kept informed of progress through regular staff and faculty meetings. Each faculty was represented on the Welfare Team. Students were informed of progress through class and year meetings and were given time to discuss issues and make suggestions. The parents were kept informed through regular newsletters and via P&C meetings.

The Welfare Team collected as much information as possible. Schools where Glasser-type systems were operating were visited and teachers from these schools were invited to speak of their experiences at staff meetings. Two DSE regional welfare consultants also assisted greatly with the development of our system. By the middle of 1987 enough information had been gathered to begin constructing our own system.

The next phase was very important. A structure had to be developed which ensured that the staff and students participated and that information flowed regularly and promptly to all concerned. Key people were targeted. The new principal of the school was enthusiastic and supportive. The next group to be targeted were head teachers. If they were committed then the system had a better than even chance of succeeding. Then followed student advisers, as they were a vital link between staff and students. Student reactions were assessed through class meetings and small group discussions.

Let's put it all together

A weekend residential conference was organised with head teachers, student advisers and the Welfare Team participating to develop a proposal for a welfare/discipline system. The broad parameters of the new system had been established by the school community. The system needed to be:

- easy to follow and easy to understand;
- positive and not punitive;
- based on a reward system;
- committed to promoting self-discipline and encouraging students to be responsible for their own behaviour;
- based on a whole-school approach to preserve consistency and universality;
- based on negotiation;
- centred on the classroom; and
- responsive to parental involvement.

The conference was held early in Term 3, 1987, and the proposal was put together for staff, student and parental discussion. Towards the end of Term 3, 1987, a staff development day was held where the final proposal was debated, discussed and eventually endorsed by the whole school community.

In a revolutionary move, the student body was given the task of formulating the new school rules around which the system would

> *operate. Some staff were sceptical about such an approach to rule-making – some felt it was akin to placing the lunatics in charge of the asylum. However, a majority of staff felt that this would give students some real power and would ensure that they were committed to the new rules. To establish the rules, about seventy percent of students across all years were surveyed. A list of rules was then taken to class meetings and a list of ten was then submitted to a staff meeting for discussion. The staff voted to accept the student-developed rules as the new school rules.*

In-servicing staff and students

Term 4 of 1987 was spent in-servicing staff, students and parents about the processes involved in the new system. It was fundamentally important that everyone involved in the system understood their responsibilities and roles within it. For teachers it was particularly important to develop negotiation skills and to ensure that the rules were applied fairly and consistently. Students were confronted with the notion that they had choices to make about their behaviour that carried positive or negative consequences.

How it works

Four key components form the basis of the system.

1. Teacher self-evaluation.
2. Positive reinforcement.
3. Negotiation.
4. Students are responsible for their own behaviour – they have choices which can result in *positive* or *negative* consequences.

If discipline problems arise in the classroom the first two steps of the system require teachers to examine what they are doing that may be contributing to the problem and to seek advice from colleagues.

When a student disrupts the class he is asked, 'What are you doing?'. If he then acknowledges his behaviour and gets back on task nothing further happens.

If the disruption continues he is directed to the 'Time-out' desk in the room and he takes no further part in the lesson – the Time-out desk has a special set of rules which must be followed by the student seated there.

The student then has the responsibility for arranging an appointment with the teacher to sit down and 'negotiate' a plan. The plan will state a set of actions the students can take to avoid getting into trouble in the future. The student is expected to follow the plan on his return to class.

The student has one week to negotiate a satisfactory plan with the teacher before he can participate in the class. If he fails to do this he is then referred to the head teacher.

A student can make up to three plans with his classroom teacher. If a fourth plan is required, he is sent to the head teacher.

When a student is placed at head-teacher level a letter is sent home to inform the parents of the situation. The student does not go to class and is instead supervised by the head teacher or placed in another teacher's classroom at the Time-out desk.

The student has one week in which to negotiate a satisfactory plan with the head teacher and the classroom teacher and so return to class. Should the student fail to do this, he is placed in the 'Blue Room' which is an isolation room supervised at all times by a teacher.

If a student is sent to the head-teacher level for a second time he is automatically placed in the Blue Room.

When a student is placed in the Blue Room the parents are notified and are asked to make an appointment to come to the school for an interview to negotiate a plan. This interview will normally involve the head teacher, a senior executive teacher, the student adviser, the parent(s), the student and, in some cases, the school counsellor.

Once a satisfactory plan is negotiated, the student is able to return to class. Should the student return to the Blue Room for a second time he may be suspended. If he is placed in the room for a third time he is automatically suspended.

In some cases, such as fighting in class, using abusive language or exhibiting threatening behaviour, a student can be placed directly in the Blue Room.

In this system there is a lot of negotiation, and at each step the student is responsible for what happens. There is always a clear choice – work it out or stay out of class.

When the system was introduced there was a fear that the 'Blue Room' would be bursting at the seams or have standing room only. This has never happened. On only two occasions has the room been under pressure when eight students were present. There are nine desks in the room.

If the students participate in establishing the system, are in-serviced on how it all works and understand the possible consequences, the problem of overcrowding in the Blue Room should never arise. This also applies to the classroom where some people thought there would need to be ten Time-out desks – each room has two. The Blue Room has, on average, two to three students placed there at any one time. During Term 1 it is usually vacant.

Positive reinforcement is a fundamental part of the system. William Glasser says, 'Catch them being good', and teachers are continually encouraged to do this through positive comments to students and by using the school's merit award system.

The discipline system became the basis for other changes

The discipline structures set up in 1988 – with many changes since – have formed the platform for all curriculum and welfare initiatives. Up until 1992, student behaviour had been modified to an extent, but further improvement was not apparent. Figures for 1990–1992 show that students removed from class for disruption accounted for 7.8 percent of the school population. Curriculum changes were instituted in 1993 that gave a much wider choice of subjects to students in Years 8, 9 and 10 and the figure dropped to 6.3 percent. In 1994 a further reduction occurred to 4.6 percent.

We are now in a position to be pro-active rather than reactive in terms of welfare and curriculum. The central point is that quality improvement occurred when the curriculum was evaluated and changes made in tandem with the discipline system. The outline of school policies that support the welfare/discipline system is shown in Figure 1 (See 'Notes'.)

What was learned?

The evolution of our welfare system has taught us a number of lessons.

1. There are no 'quick-fix' solutions to welfare problems. When we tried a 'quick-fix' approach we failed. The negative cycle had developed over a number of years and it took a number

of years to get out of it. Don't expect immediate success and make sure that people understand that it is a long-term process.

2. The change that occurs is evolutionary. It needs to become part of the school's culture. New staff and students have to be educated into it. Because it is evolutionary, adjustments have to be made on a regular basis. If part of it does not work, change it, but don't throw out the whole system. Monitoring and evaluation need to be built in to the system.

3. Any change must involve the whole school community. There was no change when we tried to impose a system from above. The year we spent in preparing the groundwork gave the system a solid foundation and its universal acceptance. People must be consulted about changes that effect the way the system operates.

4. The system and its processes must be reaffirmed on a regular basis. In the first three years the students and staff were in-serviced each semester. Later it became once a year, with constant reminders at assemblies, year meetings, staff meetings and class meetings. Rules and role statements are given to all participants in the system. (Year 7 requires special attention.)

5. People need to be convinced that students can be trusted to make informed and responsible judgements. When it came to formulating the rules the students showed maturity and common sense. They know when something needs to be changed and most of them know under what conditions they learn best.

6. It is not good enough to just look at discipline. The curriculum needs to be evaluated and changed where needed. For Canterbury Boys High School the discipline system formed the basis for curriculum change. Once discipline was under some form of control, we looked at vertical integration of classes in Years 8, 9 and 10, the establishment of an Autonomous Learning Centre, expanded subject choices and special programs such as 'Students at Risk'. These changes further improved discipline, and the introduction of a four-period day led to a re-examination of learning styles and teaching strategies.

7. Staff require constant and solid support during the implementation of changes. In-services on negotiation

(plan-making), running class meetings, identifying teaching/ learning styles and student-centred learning strategies are essential.

Evidence of change

The following student comments were taken from a school evaluation of the Glasser System, December 1993:

> The Glassier [sic] system is good because it teaches boys to be more respectful and well mannered.

> Time-out is a good thing to have as students are aware of how close they are to going to Head Teacher.

> Head Teacher plans are important as it is the step before the Blue Room and it can help students overcome their problems.

Teacher comments were taken from a staff development day – 'Reviewing Glasser', May 1994:

> On first arriving at Canterbury Boys High School thirteen years ago, I was overwhelmed by the boys' low self-esteem, racist attitudes and general sense of failure. I soon realised that these students were as talented as others but had no belief in themselves. The change since Glasser has been just as overwhelming. I now have casuals who state, as one did the other day, 'Canterbury Boys High School beats other schools hands down when it comes to a place to work'.

A teacher from a neighbouring school commented at one of their staff development days (Theme: Implementing Glasser), October 1994:

> Walking around the school (CBHS) is like walking through a library. Everyone is quiet and working.

These anecdotes give some insight into the changes that have taken place since 1988.

An examination of available statistics provides further evidence of real and significant change in students' behaviour since 1988. One indicator is to be found in the percentage of the total student population who have been placed in the 'isolation room' (Blue Room) in each year.

Graph 1 clearly indicates the change in behaviour. In 1989, nine percent of the students in the school reached the final stage

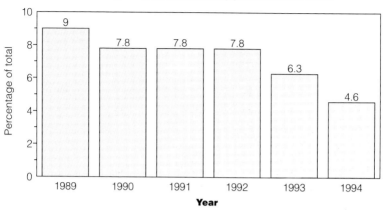

Percentage of total student body placed in Blue Room

Graph 1

of the discipline system. In 1994 this figure had fallen dramatically to 4.6 percent. The fall is even more significant when it is noted that the school's enrolment has been rising since 1992 while the number of incidents involving aggression and/or disruption has been decreasing. Furthermore, in 1989 there were twelve re-offenders (students who reached the final stage of the discipline system twice) and in 1994 there was one. In 1994 of the twenty-five students placed in the isolation room, only three were placed there because of aggressive behaviour. Before 1988 fights were an everyday occurrence in the school, they are now a rare event.

A very positive indicator is the use of the School Merit Award System. This system of rewarding students for achievement or assistance was evaluated and restructured in 1993 with a new range of high quality parchment certificates being introduced along with book voucher prizes. Students earn classroom merit awards which count towards the gaining of Certificates of Excellence (in particular subjects) and/or Certificates of Achievement (across a range of subjects). The new certificates (1000) were ordered in September 1993 and had to be re-ordered in December to take account of anticipated demand for 1994.

The rate of staff absenteeism is an excellent indicator of the stress levels being experienced by school teachers and their level of job satisfaction.

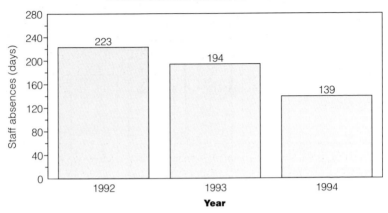

Decrease in staff absenteeism 1992–94

Graph 2

Staff absenteeism has decreased from 223 days in 1992 to 139 in 1994. Significantly, twenty percent of the allocated budget for employing relief teachers went unspent in 1994.

In an amazing contrast to views expressed in 1986, staff and students have indicated, and observers have noted, the harmonious nature of the school at all levels. Perhaps we should let others be the judge . . .

The following quotations are taken from the *Department of School Education Quality Assurance Report on Canterbury Boys High School, 1993.*

> *There was overwhelming support by all groups for the Glasser System of student welfare [which] . . . provides for negotiation, order and safety giving students responsibility for their own actions.*

> *Students could clearly articulate the processes by which the school rules were formulated and communicated. Students and parents felt that the school rules were known and fair.*

> *All groups thought that the reorganisation of curriculum had led to increased student choice and hence better learning outcomes.*

> *There is in place a range of policies supported by attitudes that have created an extremely effective welfare system.*

While at present things appear to be going smoothly, there still remains a need for maintenance and a preparedness to adjust and respond to change. In order to maintain consistency, the Welfare Team needs to be active in in-servicing new staff on procedures and 'old' staff on not cutting corners. The slogan 'Never let up on 'em' is central to maintaining the culture and initiating new members into it. The greatest danger to the system is complacency and new members who have not been a part of that process.

Fred Carosi started teaching in 1973, spending six years in a coeducational school in western Sydney. Since then he has taught in boys schools in the inner western suburbs of Sydney. He has always had an interest in boys education strategies. After his appointment to Canterbury Boys High School in 1983 he was made welfare coordinator and was a driving force behind the development and implementation of the Glasser-style welfare system at the school. He is currently the Leading Teacher at Canterbury Boys High School. Fred is married with three children, two of whom are teenage boys.

Ross Tindale started teaching in 1982 and has taught in boys high schools for the past twelve years. He developed an interest in boys education strategies as a student adviser and is currently the Head Teacher of History, PD/Health/PE and Welfare at Canterbury Boys High School. In his role as Head Teacher of Welfare he is responsible for the day-to-day running of the Glasser system, in-servicing staff and students, and generally ensuring that the system is implemented universally and consistently. Ross is married with a five-year-old son.

Breaking the
rules

Kathy Kokori, a Drama teacher in Sydney,

witnessed the transformation of relationships

in her class as students explored the divisive

issues of gender stereotyping, racism,

harassment and masculinity while developing

a new play.

Waiting for Miss

'Open the door you bitches', shouted Joe, banging loudly.

'Say please', the girls cried.

'Open up, or we'll bash the door down.'

Some of the boys, agreeable to this concept, laughed and muttered.

'Go cry to your mothers', the girls hissed.

'Don't say anything about our mothers, you Aussie sluts.'

'That's it, we're not opening the door, no way!'

'Like hell you're not.'

Turning to his side, the big boy, Joe, kicked the door viciously. His Tai Kwan Do skills had come in handy. He was, after all, the stronger, the broader, the better-looking boy, and no-one could compare. Joe yelled out again.

'Open the f——in' door!' With clenched fist, jaw twitching and flared nostrils, he looked around at the other boys, who approved of his behaviour.

The girls had locked themselves 'safely' on the inside.

I headed for the Drama room that morning in April with quite different intentions. The 'feelers' were going out into today's double period for a provocative new unit on Gender Stereotyping. The inspiration had come from a staff development workshop where we examined gender stereotypes in nursery rhymes, poetry and case studies. It was a perfect opportunity to integrate this concept with Content Areas 1, 2 and 3 as specified in the NSW Board of Studies 2-Unit Drama Syllabus. But as I approached the classroom it seemed that there was a more pressing situation to be taken care of.

Great expectations

I expected to find the students sitting in a circle on the floor (as was customary for the beginning of all Drama lessons), waiting and quietly chatting among themselves. In fact, familiarity was such that I had envisaged the dynamics of the class – the non-Anglo-Saxon boys facing the windows, huddled together, and stirring the four 'Aussie' girls about their looks, or calling them 'skips' or intimidating them with questions about their personal lives.

'Hey, Jenny, what were you and Jodie doing at the Cross last Friday night, eh?'

Sometimes the girls would laugh at their comments, and make similar remarks: 'Oh, you've made the hole in the ozone layer worse with all that hairspray you've used this morning, Joe.'

Sometimes they wouldn't. They'd sit at a distance from the boys, often on the opposite end of the room.

Robert and Trish, the exceptions, would be in some deep conversation about crystals, or auras, or a dance party that they had gone to, and how 'mad' it all was. Michael would be sitting by himself staring at a wall, playing an imaginary guitar and quietly humming a new tune his band was working on. Tony would be worrying about an English essay or warming up or taking sides with the girls. Sometimes the girls appreciated his sense of humour and his intelligent come-backs but, although they liked him, mostly they thought he was a nerd, a 'try hard'.

The 'happening'

When I arrived, the boys were yelling, banging and calling outside the locked door.

'What are you doing, boys?' I asked from about six metres up

> the corridor. I was greeted with yells and screams, foul language, hysteria, and the general ramblings of six Year 11 boys who were all trying to tell me (at the same time) their version of why Joe, the big boy, was kicking down the door.
>
> 'Miss, they won't let us in,' panted one.
>
> 'Miss, they've locked us out of the room. We didn't do nothing to them,' huffed another.
>
> 'Yeah, miss, and they slammed the door right in our face,' complained a third.
>
> 'Open the door girls,' I commanded.
>
> 'Not until they apologise,' chorused the girls, their voices filled with anger and fear.
>
> The door opened and the girls quickly took up their territory on one side of the room, while the boys stormed into the space, filling it with their presence and their righteousness. At that moment I knew that any intentions of introducing my new unit had to wait. I felt an incredible sense of hostility and tension in the room. I had to remain calm no matter how angry I was about this behaviour, for (if I was not careful) the situation could become uncontrollable.

What I was witnessing here was a 'happening', a piece of raw improvisational theatre, except that I had missed the beginning of the 'performance' and had no idea of how it would end! Scary as it was, I saw the potential here for a lesson of another sort. It was still dramatic in context, but the situation demanded a look at our actions and reactions to one another – not as characters from a play but as ourselves. The situation, which had turned into a competition of personal insults and verbal abuse (apparently as a result of an unfinished debate from the previous History lesson on the role of the family), was a potential disaster. I decided that we were going to continue with our 'happening' and somehow we would find a way of resolving it.

The importance of being heard

And so a process began. I calmly asked the group to sit down where they were standing and close their eyes.

'In a moment,' I explained, 'we are going to talk about this situation just as soon as everyone has calmed down.'

We commenced some deep breathing activities: 'On the next out-breath,' I continued, 'we are going to let out a sound which expresses the way we feel at this very moment.' I then asked them to imagine that they were dogs in a dog-pound (still with their eyes closed), and that in order to get the attention of the attendant they had to bark.

On hearing the whistle they had to stop . . . and so I let them bark for the next five minutes as loudly and as aggressively as they wanted to. And they did – barking and growling, yelping and whimpering, trying to be 'heard' by the attendant.

The rules not broken

The next step was to have the students come together in a circle. The aim was to set up some ground rules in order to resolve these conflicting behaviours of offensiveness, name-calling and aggression and try to work out ways in which we could explore what they were feeling.

Firstly, I told them there was to be no yelling and screaming. Secondly, everyone would have a chance to say something without interruption. Thirdly, no name-calling or offensive language was allowed.

And so the story unfolded. The girls didn't like the insinuations the boys were making in History about their family lives. Similarly, the boys were sick and tired of being called 'chauvinists' and 'wogs', just because they had a different opinion. We discussed the messages behind the labels that they had given each other – that of being called a 'wog,' or a 'street rat' – and discovered that such labels made them feel worthless, isolated, ugly and rejected.

One flew over the punching bag

Wanting to take the 'happening' further, I fetched the punching bag – an antistress device – from the counsellor's office. This became useful in the role-play to follow. The punching bag adopted the persona of someone from the class to whom a student wanted to express some thoughts and feelings. The student had to address the punching bag directly with the opening lines: 'Joe, when you said . . . to me, you made me feel . . .'. This verbal expression had to be followed by an appropriate action.

The improvisations continued, and although they felt anger, frustration and fury (and yelled and shrieked and let themselves cry), the girls' action was to hug the punching bag. The boys, on the other hand, yelled and projected their booming voices, and although their eyes became misty with tears, they held their breath, swallowed hard, and kicked the punching bag.

Although by now the students were much calmer and quite emotionally drained by their 'happening', they wanted to continue their improvisations when the bell rang.

'Tomorrow', I told them, 'we will write up a contract and negotiate a satisfactory resolution so that something like this does not get out of hand again.'

The following day I was greeted with a quiet lull, having asked the students whether they had thought about the negotiations. Prepared to write up the contract on the board, I asked each of them about their ideas.

'They [the boys] should stop making comments about how we live.'

'They [the girls] should stop calling us wogs.'

'We should listen to each other and work cooperatively.'

And so into their workbooks the statements went with my signature and theirs and another statement that read: 'In the event that this contract is ignored, I will be asked to learn lines at lunch time'.

Boys don't cry

Regardless of how I had intended to introduce my unit that day in April, the 'feelers' did go out.

Here was an opportunity not only to explore issues concerning gender stereotyping, but other issues just as revelant – such as harassment, relationships and masculinity. It suddenly became noticeable that for a long time now, this group had been putting down, offending, harassing and stereotyping one another. Comments were often made about effeminate behaviour; students were excluded for portraying strong masculine traits (if they were female) or weak feminine ones (if they were male). It was obvious in their role-playing – you could see it in their gestures and body language, and hear the intent in their voices.

I thought about our 'happening' at the end of that week and thought about how much contempt those students had held for each other that day. I remember feeling concerned for the safety of other students and myself a mere 153 centimetres tall. (Some of these boys were very strong and well over 190 centimetres tall.) I also remembered how frustrated the boys became as they held back their tears for fear of being labelled. Attempting to prepare some further work one night, I thought about the conditioning that society places on us and remembered the song by an English band called The Cure:

> *Boys don't cry . . .*
> *they tend to laugh about it,*
> *cover it all up with lies,*
> *they tend to laugh about it,*
> *hiding the tears from their eyes,*
> *because boys don't cry . . .*
> *boys don't cry . . .*

It was this incident that was the deciding factor for the direction the unit was going to take. We were certainly going to do some more exploration work on the issues of masculinity, harassment, gender stereotypes and sexuality.

Much ado about stereotypes

Our journey into exploring the issues of gender stereotypes, masculinity and harassment began. Over the next two weeks we searched into our childhood memories for nursery rhymes and fairy tales that typified beliefs about acceptable gender behaviour. Students remembered Cinderella and her handsome Prince, they remembered Beauty and the ferocious Beast, they thought of the ugly frog who had turned into a handsome prince when he was kissed by the 'right' girl. They wondered why Georgie Porgie ran away when the boys came out to play, and the mischief that Jack and Jill got up to 'on the hill'. Finally they remembered that 'little boys were made of frogs and snails' while 'little girls were made of sugar and spice'.

After much discussion, students were able to identify and recognise a wide range of behaviours acceptable for both men and women, regardless of cultural beliefs and differences. It was important to notice at this point that differences in attitudes and behaviour appeared largely to stem from their specific ethnic cultures. Concepts of freedom in their personal lives (and the social acceptance of other students' views and preferences within the mainstream Anglo-Saxon Australian society) vary somewhat from the concepts of behaviour that are indicative of masculinity in other cultures.

Lend me your ears

In examining the issues further, we explored a poem called 'Masculinity'. It was decided by the group to devise a performance piece based on the poem. Ideas were discussed. After a number of awareness-raising activities – case studies about friendships, discussions of acceptable behaviours and role-play – some of these ideas continued to challenge students' beliefs and attitudes. One such example of this deep-rooted difference is set out below:

> *Once, in the developmental stages of the script (taken from the ideas presented in the poem), the group was exploring ideas and developing characters. During this informal chat, it was suggested by the sensitive, intelligent boy (Tony) that he should play the waitress. This character was to be sexually harassed by one of the males in the performance piece. The others sneered at Tony's idea, especially the big boy (Joe), who muttered under his breath names like, 'fag', 'poof', 'gay', 'transvestite'. Tony's suggestion was obviously not in line with appropriate masculine behaviour, according to Joe's cultural beliefs, and Joe showed his disapproval by resorting to name-calling and labelling.*

> *'Why?' asked Tony, the boy who had the good ideas, the one that the girls liked, the one who had intentions of becoming a serious actor. 'Why', he continued, 'do the girls get to play the males, and I can't play the waitress? Besides, I'd really like to explore my acting technique', he said, 'just like Robin Williams in* Mrs Doubtfire *and Dustin Hoffman in* Tootsie.'

> *There were no reasons given, just more sneers and name-calling. The ideas flowed, plots and characters were further developed and explored. Any ideas that Tony put forward, however, were rejected and made fun of, and the other boys would make rude gestures to demean him.*

> *One day, he cracked: 'Miss, they're not listening to anything I say.' He stormed out of the room. The others watched in silence, rolled their eyes, and then laughed. Once outside, Tony burst*

into tears – tears of hurt, anger, frustration and isolation. He gave up the idea of playing the waitress and decided to explore his acting style as the drunk, instead.

To be or not to be affectionate boys

While such examples provoked discussion and provided evidence of stereotyping, the non-Anglo-Saxon boys were still afraid to hold hands in the circle, or play hug-tag and other physical, contact-type activities with one tall boy, Robert. He had long hair (sometimes pulled back into a ponytail) and so they had nicknamed him, Georgie-Porgie. (Shakespeare would have considered him an ideal boy-actor apprentice, appropriate to play women's roles in his time.) He would fling his lanky arms into the air as he pranced about the space like a 17th century fop. Other boys would subtly 'push' him out of the way if he stood too close to them. Robert's ideas were disregarded in group discussions and workshops because of his excitability, the inflection in his voice or the way that he moved. He was continually questioned about his social life and his sexuality. I reminded myself again of the conditioning ingrained into these students by their families, home environments and peers.

At times the big boy, Joe, and his friends sat in class with their arms around each other's necks, or snatched at each other's genitalia in 'brotherly affection' or rhythmically thrust their pelvises forward to mock Robert. At other times I watched Joe and his friends quite comfortably dress up in frocks and heels to play nurses, secretaries or prostitutes – or clutch handbags and try on hats for improvisations. Why had they rejected Tony's suggestion to play the waitress, I asked them one day, when they were quite comfortable playing female parts themselves? They confidently replied, 'Oh, it's OK, Miss, we're not fags, we're friends.'

After two months' work on gender issues, I wondered if institutions such as schools could have any more than a minimal impact on such deep-rooted beliefs and attitudes!

The rehearsal

By the time the script was completed and ready for rehearsal three weeks later – mid August – some remarkable changes were occurring within the group. The challenges and conflicts that had presented themselves earlier were now not major issues in class discussions and workshops. Previous behavioural patterns did not occur, and if, on the rare occasion they did, they would inform me: 'This was drama, Miss, and we're rehearsing.' Now they had a more serious matter to attend to: that of performing to an audience. And so in their efforts to produce a polished piece of theatre, they rehearsed, cooperated, listened to each other and took constructive criticism. There was no more name-calling or suggestive gestures.

A respect for each other had now formed that had not been there that day in April. When the comment was made about a male friend who was seen holding hands with another male in the city, it was the big boy, Joe, who was quick to reply: 'So what? He can do what he likes. What's wrong with that? It's his business.'

These students now faced one of the biggest challenges in their lives – that of performing in front of their peers. Their twenty-minute production, titled *Breaking the Rules*, had its debut in early September. As part of the Integrated Boys' Education Program, the play was to be performed in other schools. Its purpose was to introduce the programs which dealt with Boys Education Issues, Building Better Relationships, and Working against Harassment. In addition, our student-performers were asked to lead group discussions and participate in programs themselves. To prepare them for this experience, they were to be guided by the regional student welfare teacher and myself on how to encourage their peers.

Changes

By the end of the play's run – which took place during November – a great transformation had taken place. A deep level of understanding and recognition for each other's individuality had developed amongst the students and was now mainly observable in their conversations. I could see wonderful progress, where issues that previously had been points of contention in their interpersonal relationships were now being dealt with calmly. Their confidence and self-esteem came through a new-found responsibility: that of belonging to a group in a professional capacity. They had to do 'their' part to make sure that the production ran without hitches, and lead their groups with confidence and knowledge from their own experiences. Even their attendances improved; several teachers remarked on this with some surprise. Most importantly, they had been given a unique opportunity to explore, integrate and present a performance piece in a personal, social and cultural context. In the process, they had learnt to support each other and become friends.

It is remarkable to see them now, five months later, engaging strongly in their group presentations for the Year 12 Syllabus and highly supportive of each others' work and ideas. One boy has successfully auditioned for a major Sydney youth theatre-group, and the others look to him for inspiration on his return from Saturday workshops. This would have been unthinkable twelve months ago.

In conclusion

On reflection, my overall impression of this program is that, like any new undertaking, allowances must be made for unforeseen circumstances, such as the incident described in the beginning. Room must be made for changes and adaptations, and the teacher has to be prepared to be flexible and go with what is happening in the classroom. (In fact, the focus of this year's program will be completely different, as there are eight girls and one boy in Year 11 Drama.)

Perhaps the only change I would make in the future is to have the program compacted into a much shorter time span, as it was becoming 'boring' and tiring for some of the students to be travelling with props and costumes. In fact, when other bookings were made after our initial four performances, the students responded negatively. Realistically, the program would not have had the opportunity to travel without funding from the regional office, and this unique opportunity was a contributing factor in the program's success.

Institutions such as schools have to face a diversity of entrenched attitudes which the students bring from the home environment. The contradictions and differences in these values frequently manifest themselves in situations of conflict. It seems there is often no safe way to investigate these issues. The obvious place to work with such differences, and attitudes about difference – whether racial, class or gender – is the Drama classroom, as it provides a nonthreatening environment for intense, situational role-play. By allowing these differences to surface in their raw form we can apply a range of dramatic techniques to extend students' understanding of what is behind a situation. This will free them to explore and discover the reasons why people behave the way they do in a wider social context.

One of the key roles of the Drama teacher is to use a real-life event to provoke expression about a relevant conflict and to mediate in the follow-up discussion sessions. Teachers often feel they have a minimal impact on attitudes that stem from the home. My experience is that by using everyday events teachers can be powerful facilitators in reconciling differences and promoting tolerance.

Kathy Kokori is an experienced Drama teacher of eight years and a theatre practitioner. Cofounder of Sydney's bilingual (Greek–Australian) Take Away Theatre Inc. in 1989, Kathy has worked with professionals from the theatre industry in various areas of production including acting, stage-management, directing and technical theatre. Kathy has also assisted in the administration of the Multicultural Theatre Festival for three years, coordinating over seventeen theatre companies in stage management. Kathy enjoys doing workshops at the Actors Centre, Masterclasses, and has recently discovered the advantages of Psychodrama. Currently she is teaching Drama at a Sydney high school.

The worst class in school?

In reflecting on three different groups, *Allen Littlewood*, Head Teacher of History at Cranebrook High School, NSW, reveals that behind the behaviour of boys in class – their self-image and attitudes to learning and to girls – lie values that have a major influence on their masculine identities.

a few years ago I happened to read an article containing the simple observation that boys dominate most of a classroom teacher's time. As an inexperienced teacher, I hadn't really thought that much about it before – but it made me consider what was happening in my Year 10.1 History class. At the time the class had just started studying the suffragettes – the movement to win the vote for women at the turn of the century. I had been trying to develop the idea of what it felt like to be powerless in a society dominated by a particular group – in this case, men.

Boys – dominating the class

10H1 was a terrific class of really bright students made up of six boys and twenty-three girls. The boys sat together as a group in a corner of the room. As I considered the class it was clear that from that corner came the behavioural disruptions (such as they were); most questions for the clarification of the tasks set; the majority of answers to questions asked; and the greatest participation in general class discussion and willingness to state opinions.

> With only six boys in the class, this was a significantly dispro-
> portionate monopoly of teacher time. The parallels with the theme
> we were studying at the time seemed promising. After some
> thought I came up with the idea of a simulation game to link the
> idea of the boys dominating the class to the topic we were study-
> ing. I was interested to see what would happen.

Turning the tables

The simulation game was quite simple. In the next double period
I included a lot of oral participation and general discussion but
I only called upon girls to answer my questions or to contribute
to the discussion. At first the boys patiently conformed and
accepted my disapproval when they called out instead of raising
their hands. Frustration began to register in comments like,
'Come on, I know the answer,' and escalated to statements like,
'He's only asking the dumb girls,' and, 'That was a stupid
answer.'

Behavioural disruption increased as talk between the boys
became louder and deliberately more intrusive. Fidgeting escalated and books and pens began to fly. I intervened periodically
but mostly ignored the performance.

> The lesson came to a point when all the boys but one had com-
> pletely signed off. It was clear that the last boy, Stewy, was not
> going to be defeated. He began to bang his fist on the table, then
> banged the table against other tables and chairs and stood up, all
> the time thrusting his hand in the air indicating that he wanted
> to answer questions.
>
> The final straw came when he stormed over in front of me,
> waved his hands in my face and yelled, 'What do I have to do to
> get you to listen to me?'
>
> Now that was a really good question. I certainly hadn't antici-
> pated Stewy's reaction. His question confronted a number of
> issues that I had not previously considered. During this whole
> lesson, in fact, the reaction of the boys provided me with a
> number of unexpected insights.

A lesson in domination

In the debriefing discussion that followed I explained to the class,
in the context of the topic we were studying, what I was doing

and why. The girls recognised and identified with the idea of not getting a fair go immediately and this provoked some lively discussion. This time the boys were allowed to contribute and they confirmed that it clearly didn't feel good when the boot was on the other foot. Having set up, in a real sense, the idea that some groups dominate and others don't like it, this lesson provided a good staging point for the remainder of the topic about the suffragettes. I also vowed to be more aware in my teaching of the needs of girls and to include them more, especially in questioning and discussion.

The 10H1 simulation-game lesson had confirmed what the article that provoked it had stated – that boys did appear to dominate lessons. The lesson had also given me an opportunity to develop the content issues involved in the topic that the class had been studying. In addition the experience had given me two quite unanticipated insights into the teaching of history to boys and the nature of adolescent masculinity.

Boys' values and their behaviour

> *In the debriefing part of the lesson, two repeated statements by the girls were, 'You boys think you know it all', and, 'You boys think you're more important than us'. Jokingly, but I suspect with a shade of real belief, boys replied, 'That's because it's true'.*

Although they were generalising, the girls were stating their reactions to a significant value that they saw as characteristic of the boys' behaviour. The girls believed that the boys saw themselves as innately superior and, by implication, the girls as inferior. To the girls, the boys' sarcastic reply served only to confirm this.

Quite apart from recognising the basic inequality that this implied (and the implications for equality of opportunities), this exchange between the boys and girls provoked in me some significant questions. What were the values that the boys held about themselves as individuals, their status in relation to the girls and in relation to conforming to the expectations of the other boys? What values did the boys hold about the status of girls? How did the behaviours of the boys demonstrate the values that they held? If the values that the boys held led to destructive behaviours how could those values be challenged and modified?

Clearly the values that were behind the behaviours of the boys were influencing their masculine identities and I needed to consider those values in my teaching.

The cycle of frustration and bad behaviour

In relation to the experiences of boys, the 10H1 lesson underlined another important point for me as a teacher. Issues of self-esteem and valuing the individual are most important in developing adolescent masculinities. The lesson reversed the then existing status and identity of the individuals in the class.

In their attempts to return the lesson to 'normal' some of the boys, and especially Stewy, couldn't get the attention that they were used to within acceptable norms of behaviour. So they stepped outside what they knew I thought was reasonable; and these were academically able and well-mannered kids.

I could easily see the frustration and alienation that less academically able and socially disadvantaged students must feel in classrooms where the competition and need for positive attention is much greater. This would inevitably lead to poor behaviour, poor performance, and dissatisfaction with (and non-participation in) schooling. Teachers get stressed, punishment becomes a preoccupation, negative associations build, student self-esteem takes a battering and everyone is the loser. In the 10H1 lesson, the boys thought that they held no worth or value within the existing frameworks so they pursued an identity and attention outside the framework.

Valuing boys

At the time, the main objectives of the 10H1 lesson related to developing the content of the topic being studied. Subsequently, however, I have attempted to integrate into my teaching a consistent focus on two issues – teaching values to boys and valuing boys for who they are. This has not been easy because some adolescent masculine identities thrive on opposition and destructive self-images.

Since becoming a head teacher I have always allocated myself classes containing the less able and behaviourally difficult students. Few other teachers willingly volunteer to take these difficult groups. By taking them myself I have fewer occasions where I have to intervene as a third party in situations of confrontation between students and teachers. It's probably no surprise that the majority of students in these classes are boys. The 10H1 lesson reinforced my developing belief that I needed to establish positive rapport and supportive working relationships with students in my classes if I was to influence them as effective learners in general and in my subject specifically.

'The worst class in school'

A recent Year 8 class (all boys and which I had allocated to myself) had the most extreme behaviours. Every one of them was suspended from school at least twice in the course of the year. Most had difficult home lives. They stole, fought, swore at teachers, assaulted, victimised and generated unpleasant smells. Two of the boys had been suspended for deliberately disguising and exploding a detonator on the good side of a student who was already deaf in one ear. One teacher called them 'animals' to their faces. Most teachers dreaded taking them. The boys individually didn't like being in the class. They called each other 'animals' or any other hurtful or sexualised insult that they could think of. As a group, however, they showed a remarkable collective pride in being, 'the worst class in the school'. Their behaviour certainly complemented and reinforced this opinion of their status.

Using praise

For me, the priority was to establish a strong interpersonal rapport by being genuinely and unrelentingly positive. Every opportunity was exploited. Every lesson started with a positive greeting for each boy. Most misbehaviours were dealt with by making statements like, 'Because we respect each other in this class we don't do that'.

Compliance with work expectations was met with personal attention, private and public compliments, and recommending to close peers that if they looked at a particular student's work they would get some great ideas. Merit cards were only given out as a celebration of excellent work and participation – never as a reward for good conduct.

I always greeted them when I saw them in the playground or going between lessons. When other teachers came into the room I told them that this was the best class and that they should look

> at some of the work they were doing, or pointed out work that had been pinned on the wall. Every lesson ended with a statement such as, 'That was great', 'You did well', 'What a great class'.

Becoming accepted

At first the boys were suspicious and certainly confused. None of them could handle being complimented or greeted by a teacher who seemed to *want* them to be in his class. It was quite difficult at times to maintain the positive emphasis (or just to maintain an even temper), given some of the misbehaviour that the boys got up to. At times I felt thoroughly discouraged. My personal esteem was regularly shaken. On many occasions for example, students deliberately abused and hit other students, and I was powerless to stop it. On other occasions they verbally abused me in a fit of temper because I had insisted that they carry out a reasonable instruction. Only a few of my colleagues could understand why I persisted with reinforcing the positive when it would have been so much easier to just give up.

However, through persistence, the boys gradually came to see me as genuine and caring. In this situation some trust emerged and they increasingly accepted me as a more significant person in their lives. This was also the experience of another head teacher who also used the same approach with the class.

By the end of the year they were still no angels. However, increasingly they were more willing to pay attention, behave themselves and therefore gain from the learning experiences offered. Being valued as individuals had a great impact on the boys' self-esteem and self-respect. This was quite a significant development for them. They now recognised themselves as capable of being responsible and able to relate maturely with other people – important lessons on the road to becoming better men.

Being valued

Placing value on the individual is not specific to the History classroom. Effective teachers in every school develop classroom practices and operate at interpersonal levels which positively influence student self-esteem. Whole-school welfare programs are built around this idea. From the point of view of a History teacher, however, for students to learn history they first have to *choose* to learn and participate. In the case of the boys in the Year 8 class, being valued by the teacher was one of the factors influencing that decision.

Experiences such as these clearly identify for me that the need for boys to feel valued and recognised is an important element of their self-mage and self-esteem. However, dealing with some of the values that underpin boys' behaviours presents a quite different problem in the classroom. The teaching of History gives us an important opportunity to challenge and influence the values of boys. In teaching with this objective we can confront stereotypes and positively model emerging masculine identities.

Challenging values

> *During 1994 I taught a Year 9 class an elective topic called, 'Arrows, Spears, and Swords'. The apparent promise of the title resulted in twenty-two boys and three girls taking the unit. In one lesson I introduced, as an historical source, a statement made by General Sheridan about American Indians that, 'The only good Indian I ever saw was dead'. This immediately provoked from a number of the boys comments such as, 'Yeah! He got that right', and, 'They should have done that to our abo's'. In the past when I had significantly less experience – I would have confronted these students publicly with the racist, insensitive and obscene nature of their comments. The results (in similar cases) were that students reacted by defending their statements or by brooding about being made to feel guilty. On occasions when I opened up racist comments to class discussion, the same effect was created: a reinforcement of the racial intolerance which provoked the discussion. Either response would have reinforced the inherent values and attitudes behind the statements that the boys had made because their self-respect and their credibility and identity within their peer group was at stake. The last thing I wanted to do was to force the boys to publicly defend an aspect of their masculinity. This, as a way of influencing change, has never worked in my experience.*

Instead of publicly denigrating the boys' statements, I directed the class back to the Sheridan document and asked them a series of questions. What did they consider Sheridan thought about himself compared with the Indians? What did Sheridan think about the value of human life? What might be General Sheridan's attitude to power? What might be Sheridan's attitude towards Indian women and children? What might Sheridan think about people who are different? Why might Sheridan think these things? What would people think if Sheridan made similar statements about a group of people today?

These questions raised the same issues that I wanted the boys to think about but allowed them to consider them in an historical context. The questions confronted Sheridan's values not the boys'. The answers established a climate of what the class collectively regarded as reasonable attitudes to hold about issues that had been raised. I did notice that the offending boys had not offered much by way of answers but were listening.

Redefining values of masculinity

I did a similar 'values' diagnosis' when the class had completed some research on the Sand Creek Massacre in which 300 Indians, mostly women and children, had been slaughtered and their corpses mutilated by a group of US cavalrymen. I repeated the exercise after we had looked at Custer's Last Stand and discussed Indian as well as white values of that time. By the time we began examining the evidence that described the so-called, 'Battle of Wounded Knee', the boy who had made the previous statement about the Aborigines said (without prompting or appropriate caution), 'Shit, those whites were bastards, weren't they?'.

While I may not have approved of his means of expression, this boy had genuinely learned by internalising and personalising the new information about values and attitudes. He had abandoned one aspect of his masculine self-image without the threat or humiliation of public denigration.

I have worked with History teachers who have a major preoccupation with just teaching factual knowledge or content. Fortunately for most, however, there is at least an equal emphasis on the development of a wide range of history skills. I have come across very few teachers who actively focus on the teaching of values – probably because values are not assessed. The above example, however, confirms for me that few subjects are as well placed as History to actually challenge the values and conventions that produce the masculine stereotypes which damage boys and, later, men.

One of the lessons of history is that confrontation often leads to war. History teachers are well positioned to encourage boys to assess the value structures that underpin the behaviours and identity of boys today – without the direct confrontation that often happens. One way is to have students identify, evaluate and challenge the values and attitudes which are contained in the sources, artifacts and events of the past. This is a significant step towards developing true historical empathy in students. Boys with empathy for people in the past have a better chance of translating that into their behaviours and their relationships with people in their own lives.

Building relationships

Now with the benefit of a decade more experience, as I think back to the 10H1 lesson in which I set out to ignore the boys who had been dominating the class – I realise what a potentially risky thing I had done. When boys perform 'like boys', they are essentially creating identities for themselves as a way to gain more personal or social power. Why else would they behave in particular ways? As a result, playing with a person's emotional commitment to an identity can be very unpredictable. The last thing I, or the other class members, expected Stewy to do was to physically confront me as a teacher. That's not an element of masculine identity that any of us wants to encourage. It remains, however, a good illustration of a process of alienation and reaction which I suspect is played out in classrooms everywhere, and manifests itself in a huge range of noncompliant, violent and attention-seeking behaviours.

I am convinced that History teachers have a unique opportunity to challenge the range of values that often underpin boys' images of themselves and their resulting behaviours. This can be achieved without publicly damaging the self-esteem of students by confronting those same values with the benefit of the distance of events from the past. There are many ways to achieve this. However, perhaps two of the key prerequisites are for teachers to actually *like* working with boys and to ensure they build strong, positive interpersonal relationships with them. After all, boys are only human.

Allen Littlewood is Head Teacher (History) at Cranebrook High School. He has had wide experience in the professional development of teachers within his school and across Metropolitan West Region in areas such as History Curriculum delivery, Executive Development, Student Welfare and Teaching and Learning using the Accelerative Learning methodology. During November, 1994, he copresented a work-in progress report, 'Not more Great Men, Just Better Men: Teaching History to Boys', at the Australian Association for Research in Education Men's Workshop in Newcastle. His hope is that his two children, Erin and Samuel, will inherit a world which values equity, compassion and tolerance.

Can I use the word 'gay'?

Maria Pallotta-Chiarolli, a teacher, author and
leading proponent of teaching social justice issues in
schools, describes the challenges of introducing
homophobia in boys schools and the rewards that
can follow engaging students with such an
important issue.

'They treat you like you're subhuman or something'

After looking around to make sure others weren't listening, a student in one of my first classes quietly asked if he'd get into trouble if he used the word 'gay' in his essay. 'Well, it depends on how you're going to use the word 'gay',' I answered, and followed this with an explanation of homophobia, language use and context.

From then on, I often began my classes each year with 'This will be a nonracist, nonsexist, nonhomophobic classroom'. It was always the last one that got the looks of puzzlement. A confident 'It-may-be-the-first-day-of-the-year-but-I'm-letting-you-know-I'm-the-one-that-will-either-help-break-or-make-your-class' hand would shoot up and ask, 'What's homo, homo, whatever you said?'.

A few brave laughs in the classroom, and I would thank him for 'being so honest and asking a question that I'm sure many students would like answered'. This ensured he was now on side and I could introduce my first short lesson on homophobia: what it was and why it would be inappropriate in my classes.

I found that in the first year or two students would test this part of the classroom contract more than the other two. It became obvious I was serious, as I was ready to follow up misdemeanours alongside and in the same ways that I dealt with other social injustices. With the same faces popping up in my classes year after year, it became less necessary to define homophobia and there was less student testing.

Thus, antihomophobia became an accepted norm in my classroom. This was proven regularly. For example, a student in my marginal, 'remedial English' class, which comprised some of the most difficult boys in the school, suddenly shouted out one day, 'You know what? Prejudice is like how we're supposed to be the thicko class but we're really good at all sorts of things. But some teachers and other kids don't want to know. So it's like if you're gay, they treat you like you're thick or subhuman or something.' Crescendos of applause, including my own, followed.

As my teaching career progressed, it became increasingly obvious that on-the-spot interventions and mainstreaming approaches were the most effective ways of challenging homophobia. Implementing antihomophobia strategies did not mean designing and teaching a two-week unit for the classroom and then forgetting about the issue for the rest of the year. Specific teaching units were a significant part of the larger but not impossible task of shifting school culture in relation to issues of gender, race, sexuality and other social justice issues.

'It's just part of everything else'

Shifting school culture in relation to homophobia means developing a perspective which reflects on everything we do both inside and outside the classroom. This does not mean homophobia and homosexuality have to be mentioned constantly. As with antiracism and antisexism, antihomophobic principles and objectives will inform what we teach, why we are teaching it and the methods used in that teaching. In other words, how will homophobia be included and incorporated into existing policies, practices and perceptions? What is already in our school culture that can be put to use in challenging homophobia?

Research shows that schools which adopt an incorporative framework or inclusive approach to issues of homosexuality are far more successful than isolated teachers working without structural, administrative and peer support. Nevertheless, research also indicates that this whole-school approach is rarely arrived at without the determined, persistent, and at times, painful efforts and experiences of those isolated teachers who gradually find themselves acting like pebbles thrown into a pond – the ripples spread out further and further.

Two Catholic boys schools – not including our school – were recently faced with a gay male staff member dying of AIDS. One school handled the death, the disease and the sexuality of the teacher with respect – a large school presence at the funeral and other public responses such as in school newsletters. Pastoral care lessons were given over to discussion and learning. Any homophobia or AIDS-phobia was dealt with seriously. In fact, the work that had been done before the teacher's death was now resumed with even more participation from staff, students and parents. The other school tried to silence the disease and the sexuality and briefly acknowledged the death. However, rumours spread. Parents were distressed: some were loudly homophobic; others were upset that the school had not taken up its Christian responsibility to challenge AIDS-phobia and homophobia. Staff and some students were being confronted with homophobia from other students. There was frustration in relation to appropriate responses as there had been no direction from the administration. The levels of bullying and other forms of harassment increased dramatically.

'It's part of the school rules'

I have not heard of any school which has a specific antihomophobia policy. What is proving useful and effective is to incorporate homophobia into existing policies such as social justice, behavioural management, curriculum development, harassment, yard behaviour, language use, pastoral care, mission statements, the set of rules and regulations often listed at the front of school diaries, often placed on a classroom wall and often discussed and agreed upon with students as part of the classroom behaviour guidelines. Thus, a simple statement such as the following in an existing harassment policy is useful: 'Any form of harassment based on references to homosexuality is contrary to the school's values of social justice and respect for the individual.'

Having policies which are intended to cover homophobia and are seen to do so means that administrative support is available for teachers and students both before and after incidents involving homophobia. At the time of the publication of *Someone You*

Know, my book about an HIV-positive, gay, male teacher who had taught at the school, the school policies must have been ready and waiting! I found out months later that a handful of parents had contacted the administration and were calmly and clearly dealt with 'in the light of the Catholic ethos of the school'. I was not even told! It had been 'an administrative matter' that did not require my needing to justify or explain anything. One persistent parent was invited to contact the Catholic Education Office or Church Office if further clarification was required. I did later learn of how a couple of letters were received and responded to without fuss. Thus, a whole-school approach and ideally a whole-system approach diffuses potential conflicts and downplays the supposedly controversial or scandalous nature of an issue.

'We're doing antihomophobia stuff'

I found the following two questions useful in curriculum development and resource selection:

- How can students be guided to be critical of representations that normalise homophobic practices?
- How can students be guided to empathise with the experience of and resistance to homophobic discrimination?

Most of my antihomophobic work with boys was done in the English classroom. Social Studies, Australian Studies and History Studies are three other areas where much work can be done. What became apparent was not only the need for specific anti-homophobic material, but how material that didn't even address homosexuality could be very useful, particularly if it dealt with some form of social injustice, or if it negated or ignored homophobia or homosexual/bisexual persons. For example, when my students were asked to write scripts about harassment and perform them in groups, I would want different groups to examine various forms of harassment. Thus, they would be guided to include homophobic harassment. Part of the challenge I gave all groups was to deal with their topics devoid of stereotyping. Early drafts of plays were monitored for such 'harassing stereotypes'. In this way, much antihomophobic learning occurred as part of the planning, writing and rehearsal process, and prevented the final performances from inciting disruption from the rest of the class.

Texts on Australian gay, lesbian and bisexual history provide important factual data that previous history books tended to silence. In relation to international history, there are history texts which uncover details omitted in mainstream (read: homophobic) history texts. For example, when studying the Nazi concentration camps of World War II, I would guide students to recognising the omissions in their school texts of gay and lesbian persecution and would provide material from other texts. A recently published poignant short story on the experiences of a gay Jewish man losing his lover in a concentration camp would be an ideal narrative to accompany factual studies. Likewise, studies of societies such as ancient Rome and Greece, as well as pre-Western or pre-colonial societies such as the Native Americans, Australian Aboriginals and Hindu cultures provide diverse knowledge of other concepts of 'normal' and 'abnormal'.

Gaining access to antihomophobic texts is becoming easier. Various specialist libraries, bookshops and organisations can be found in most capital cities.

Sometimes all that is required is a mention of some fact or detail to broaden students' minds to possibilities and realities that have been denied or silenced. For example, in Economics, what else do we know about Maynard Keynes, the brilliant economic theorist? What do we know about other productive members of our society in the past and in the present: artists, writers, scientists, sporting heroes? It has become standard practice to discuss the significance of gender, race, ethnicity, geographical and historical location in biographies and yet homosexuality and bisexuality are often silenced or seen as of no relevance. Providing a homosexual or bisexual identity to persons not only erodes the perception of the nonexistence of nonheterosexual persons throughout history and in contemporary society, but allows for role modelling for gay students and a breaking of stereotypes of who would be a gay person. This is all part of shifting school culture where the 'unmentionable' becomes part of daily teaching practice.

Once groundwork had been covered, one of the most successful events at our school was inviting a lesbian in her early twenties to conduct workshops and chat to a class of senior students. When asked to anonymously comment on the session, eighteen of the twenty students said they had found it easy to talk to her about parents, jobs, study, being in love, fashions, gender roles, and her being a lesbian and the homophobia she often had to deal with. The two negative assessors both said they had liked her but felt uncomfortable with the way 'she was so open and proud to be a lesbian'. After the session, news travelled through the school fairly fast, but we had done enough ground-work, for we did not hear one negative comment from students. However, some staff were rather stressed at possible ramifications with parents. This did not eventuate. A few staff had found it highly inappropriate. But we had proven a point: how accepting students could be; how useful the exercise had been. In fact, Kerry had been so successful that future classes wanted to meet her. We clearly explained to students that what we had done was considered inappropriate by some members of the staff and so the concern with what homophobia does in terms of silencing, denial, discrimination was a useful discussion exercise in itself. Indeed, one student came to some of my University of South Australia lectures and seminars – with full parental approval – in order to listen to Kerry and a gay male present their work-shops.

'I see things differently now'

> I know that thirty years of learning patriarchal values can be undermined in thirty seconds: and the world never looks the same again.
>
> Dale Spender

That's all it took sometimes: just a few words, a question, some facts, an honest response to a concern, a poster, a song, a personal anecdote, and students no longer accepted that homophobia was normal and justifiable.

Shifting staff and student perceptions in relation to homosex-uality means undertaking various forms of awareness-raising strategies. Posters and displays in relation to equal opportunities and social justice can include antihomophobia alongside anti-racism and antisexism. Public events like assemblies and publicity pieces such as newsletters are effective shifters of cul-tural mores and expectations via the use of language and content. One school in London holds assemblies which have marked International Women's Day, Martin Luther King Jr's birthday, World AIDS Day, May Day, Nelson Mandela's release from prison, and Lesbian and Gay Pride Week.

Shifting the school culture in relation to masculinity will create openings for work on antihomophobia. Broadening the extra-curricular activities to encourage student participation in areas other than football and soccer allowed for students to join the drama club, art club, writers' club. The first boys to join the drama club and put on a school performance were subjected to homophobic intimidation on buses and in the yard. The school dealt with this in various ways: constant encouragement of the boys' participation, intervening in the homophobic harassment either immediately and directly or through curriculum support, and giving public space to these boys alongside the football team and soccer team at assemblies and in newsletters. The intimidation diminished. Instead, after the success of the first school production, students were queuing to join in. We knew we had made progress when we staged *A Midsummer Night's Dream* with our boys sewing and wearing fairy costumes and all sorts of cross-dressing, and hardly a homophobic ripple was heard! We had done some groundwork, of course, in the study of all-male acting troupes in Shakespeare's time and the use of make-up by men at various points in history and in various cultures, again encouraging students to consider social attitudes and gender roles as indicative of a particular society, place and time.

Teachers themselves are very influential in shifting perceptions. A boys school principal invited me to speak to his Year 12 Religious Education class. After introducing me, he told the boys he had grown up thinking of homosexuality as a taboo subject, and later only had access to the vicious stereotypes. He said he was still needing to 'understand and accept' and he would be sitting in on the class alongside them, wanting to learn. This presentation of his own position cleared the air for some honest questions, debate, and effective learning. At our own school, a few colleagues would talk to the boys about how they had been extremely homophobic at school and how it took years of adulthood and mixing with gay people before their prejudices were shifted. This honesty meant that students could see that they were not being targeted as 'bad' for being homophobic, or being made fun of for being ignorant about homosexual issues. Instead, we focused on why they had such opinions. Where were they coming from? Wasn't it unfair that they weren't being given relevant information and experience upon which to base their perceptions of people?

Teachers who deal with homophobia by nonintervention, joking and laughing along, making careless statements, or covering their own discomfort through discomforting statements are colluding with homophobia. A popular teacher at a boys school told me that the homophobic comments in his classroom had made him uneasy and so he had chosen 'what looked like the easy way out and joined in'. This had led to an escalation of the homophobia and he was now greatly disturbed and wondering what to do. My suggestion was to be honest with the students by explaining his own discomfort with the issues, to discuss his own upbringing and schooling in relation to these topics, and then to negotiate with his class how they could all 'work together on this tough issue'. He found that his honesty at first resulted in derisive put-downs – 'the kind I would've previously made to them' – before significant shifts in language use and attitudes began to occur.

A lesbian recalled the following incident in a Religious Education class:

> . . . someone asked if love between people of the same sex was wrong.
>
> The teacher answered that he 'did not want to condemn anyone but on the other hand, a plug and a plug and a socket and a socket'. It was never mentioned again.

This kind of response can be very detrimental and hurtful. It fails to deal with the question of love, equates lesbian and gay relationships only with sex, and the opportunity for a serious and useful discussion about relationships is lost.

I often had students telling me how they 'camped it up' for one male teacher just to hear him make homophobic comments about them. This would make other students laugh at him and call him a 'poofter-basher'. They liked the way he 'made a fool of himself', pretending to be 'so macho and a real man'. Although I did not condone their behaviour, it frustrated me that this teacher could not see how his homophobia was creating havoc in his classroom with boys who were very aware of his prejudice. I later found out that one of the boys in the group had indeed been gay and his friends had tried to show him their support through their behaviour towards the teacher in a way that wouldn't reveal their friend's sexuality to either the teacher or the rest of the class.

Ex-students who identified themselves as gay told me how they appreciated the teachers who did intervene. One ex-student told me about one teacher of non-English speaking background who would 'have fits' if any racist comments were made in class but was the first to make homophobic comments and enjoy homophobic jokes at the expense of boys 'who couldn't play football and soccer the way he wanted'.

'Are you a lesbian, Ms Chiarolli?'

How do we respond when our own sexuality is challenged or queried? Although it is still difficult for gay, lesbian and bisexual teachers to be open at school, judging from the impact Jon's posthumous 'coming out' (through my book) had on parents and students and from discussions with openly gay teachers in some Australian schools, I believe this form of personal contact is very powerful and I hope more and more teachers will be able to 'come out' in their schools. On the other hand, I would encourage heterosexual teachers not to be so defensive about their own sexuality. Phrases like, 'I'm not gay myself, of course, . . .'; 'I can't imagine myself as gay . . .'; 'Thank God I'm not talking about myself here . . .' still convey fear and discomfort. By not using their heterosexuality as a defence or protection, teachers are role modelling comfort and strength in the face of homophobic harassment.

Every now and again a student would state or intimate that I was a lesbian. I would neither deny nor affirm. Instead, I'd make comments such as, 'And if I am, what does that mean to you?', 'Thank you. I think being seen as a lesbian is quite a compliment, for lesbians have so much to teach straight women', 'It's great you don't have stereotypical views about lesbians! Some guys would look at my long hair, my make-up and clothes, and never think I could be a lesbian!'. I remember a senior student rushing up to me one lunchtime: 'I'm going to punch that idiot's face in! He just called you a dyke!'.

'What are you so upset about? And I don't appreciate that macho aggression on my behalf.'

'But, but I want to do it for you, for your reputation! You're not a dyke.'

'But what's wrong with being a dyke? Let him think that. Now if he says it in a homophobic way in the classroom, I'll deal with it. But I bet he won't, because he knows it doesn't bother me. But I do care about the way you think you can solve problems by punching people in the face! If you need to protect my honour, go back and tell him that you don't think being called gay or a lesbian is anything dishonourable to me.'

'You're promoting homosexuality'

A simple poster started it: the silhouettes of two men facing each other, their arms around each other's shoulders. The accompanying text spoke of how strange it was that two men touching each other was considered unusual when thousands of media images of men killing each other was considered normal. I put it up in the staff room as it indicated one of the issues I was addressing: the acceptance of aggression and conflict as part of the construction of 'normal' masculinity. I returned to school the next day to find an anonymous white paper pinned to the poster declaring: 'You are promoting homosexuality in the school'. This was followed by two consecutive days of anonymous papers taped to the wall near my desk with outdated Catholic Church dogma and Biblical quotes on homosexuality.

The reality is that there will be resistance, but would it be acceptable to say, 'I'm not going to study sexism/racism in my school because the kids/parents/peers are too sexist/racist?'. Resistance from staff, students and parents is often framed in the accusations of 'promoting homosexuality' and being 'anti-heterosexual'. This resistance is greatly decreased or prevented if the emphasis in the work teachers do is on the broader themes such as social justice, marginality, prejudice and discrimination, and lesson plans and materials exemplify this integration through a variety of resources, methodologies and contents. Homophobia is seen to be part of a greater picture that the school undertakes as part of its responsibility in the intellectual, personal and social development of students. This is where the incorporation of homophobia into school policies can play a crucial role.

Resistance from parents is greatly decreased if they do not feel as if their values are being ignored and views they feel uncomfortable with are being forced onto their children. Resistance from students is greatly decreased if they do not feel as if they are being coerced to adopt a particular stance or being harangued as 'homophobes'. Parents can be reassured that students are encouraged to clarify the difference between voicing a personal opinion or preference, and voicing a prejudice and oppressing others. They must feel free to voice a personal opinion and be guided in examining where that opinion comes from and on what it is based, rather than being forced into silence so that significant issues never get aired, or be incited into further homophobic resistance as a way of rebelling against the teacher. I also found that student resistances were increasingly met and responded to by other students as the environment was made a safe space to discuss issues and affirm alternative ways of knowing and being. Here are two examples from my classes:

> Student 1: *'But if a boy is brought up with two lesbians as parents, how's he going to develop into a real boy? You need a man around.'*

> Student 2 (popular school champion soccer player): *'My mother raised me all by herself because my dad left her when I was a baby. And I'm the school's best soccer player and I grew up with mostly women and that's why I reckon I'm also a nicer guy.'*

> Student 1: *'I don't mind gays and lesbians but I don't think they should be parents. Their kids grow up weird.'*

> Student 2 (a popular boy highly respected amongst peers): *'My auntie's a lesbian and she's raised my three cousins and some of youse hang out with them. Are they weird?'*

Often, there was laughter and applause from others, keeping the classroom atmosphere positive and full of energy. The self-proclaimed 'homophobes' would reconsider as their peers opened the closets in their own lives. And I would just sit silently on the desk and feel it wasn't worth adding anything. The students were guiding each other.

Over the years, it seems to me that teachers who have the most success in dealing with issues such as sexism and homophobia try to develop strong relationships with students through their genuine concern and liking for them, and are not willing to resort to violence and verbal abuse as a way of 'controlling' the students. They also endeavour to present themselves not only as teachers but also as persons with lives outside the school, and as individuals questioning and reflecting upon their own values in relation to people and social justice. They try to be very open with students in relation to feelings and sensitivity, as well as being firm in expectations and consequences for misbehaviour. They will also try to be honest with students in relation to their discomfort with particular unjust school and societal rules and expectations.

'You're going against the Church'

As a teacher in a Catholic school, I was sometimes told I was being antiChristian in teaching antihomophobia. In my work with teachers and administrators of Catholic schools, I find many who wish to begin challenging homophobia but fear the professional and personal consequences. Are we being cowed into inaction by some homophobic Church leaders? Are we being prevented from finding points of connection with aspects of our religious beliefs from which to begin developing antihomophobic initiatives? Here is one example of a useful statement. A Vatican document stated in 1986:

> It is deplorable that homosexual persons have been and are the object of violent malice in speech and action. It reveals a kind of disregard for others which endangers the most fundamental principles of a healthy society. The intrinsic dignity of each person must always be respected in word, in action and in law.

This is clearly an antihomophobic statement that is useful in dealing with parental, staff and student resistance.

Catholic schools are actually not carrying out their Christian mission statements if they do not address homophobia. I would respond to any personal criticism by saying I was being unChristian if I didn't challenge homophobia. When the realities are that gay-bashers are coming from private boys schools, that boys in Catholic schools are facing homophobic harassment, that there are HIV-positive and/or gay students and teachers in Catholic schools who are feeling isolated and alienated, and HIV-positive and/or gay adults who left Catholic schools with low self-esteem and minimal sexuality and HIV/AIDS education, Catholic schools need to question whether 'the Catholic ethos' is actually a reality in their school communities.

'It's in the too-hard basket'

Basically, as with the pursuit of other social justice issues, the more of us who take up this basket, the lighter it will get. And how do I know challenging homophobia works? There were several indications:

- Students intervening in each other's homophobic language and attitudes in class was very powerful. Likewise, meetings with ex-students confirmed the success of at least one point of teacher intervention in a classroom.

> *Your English lessons were so important to me. It was the first time I ever heard an adult say something good about how I was secretly feeling. But I couldn't tell you then. I was too shy and I thought the other guys might find out. But I kept on reading and learning and now everything's alright.*

- Students who defined themselves as homophobic were able to reconsider their positions:

> *I think I will somehow get rid of my prejudice against homosexuals by trying to see what it would be like to be one and have the world against you. Like Atticus said, we have to get into their shoes to find out how life is really treating them.*

> *If I were to get to know someone with AIDS or who is gay, I think I would be able to change my prejudice . . . seeing he's alright after all.*

- I have received positive letters and chatted with enthusiastic students and teachers from various schools in Australia using *Someone You Know* as a text. As one male student euphemistically wrote to me after reading *Someone You Know*:

> *The initial reading of the book proved very enjoyable, as there was no mention of homosexuality or AIDS. It was not until the third chapter that I realised Jon was gay. Personally, this posed a problem. I regret to say I have always had an 'immense dislike' toward homosexuals. Yet, after a little self-deliberation, I decided to continue, although determined not to enjoy it. To my surprise, I was glad I persevered.*

- A gruff adolescent male voice on my answering machine late one night stunned me with his more blunt approach:

  I'm ringin' cos I just finished yer book about AIDS and poofters – uh, gay men – and it's made me do a lotta thinkin' and I feel like a f——in' shit for having bashed one. It sure won't happen again. Yeah, well, thanks.

Maria Pallotta-Chiarolli has taught in a Catholic boys secondary school for eleven years, has lectured in universities and is currently undertaking PhD studies. She is a consultant, particularly in education, on issues concerning ethnicity, gender, sexuality and HIV/AIDS. Maria is the author of *Someone You Know* (a biography which presents the impact of AIDS and homophobia on human relationships); her other writings are widely published in journals and anthologies. As Gender and Equity Officer for the C.E.O. (1992-1993), she developed the Gender and Equity Policy for South Australian Catholic Schools.

Working with boys and masculinity

There *are* ways of getting around the resistance boys have to dealing with masculinity and their own behaviour – and of moving on to the important task of raising their self-awareness. *Rollo Browne*, an independent consultant to schools on boys' education, reports from the frontline.

The girls were seated on one side, stony faced; the boys on the other, egging each other on. It was a double period – a Year 9 Personal Development session in a school with a strong surfie culture. The topic was 'Sexuality and Harassment'. It was about halfway through the session. The girls had gone silent. The boys were doing all the talking but there was not much sense or empathy from them.

On impulse I asked, 'Do you know about the Anita Cobby case?' This was a brutal rape and murder then in the news. 'They got a hunting knife and stuck it up her and twisted it around her c——', came the deadpan reply.

I was floored. They knew more about it than I did, in graphic horror-movie style. I struggled on about violence and humiliation of women in harassment and rape. More than half the boys admitted to seeing porn videos, but our discussion could not get beyond their boasting and exaggerating for audience effect. By the end, I had the sinking feeling that instead of challenging the values and attitudes of this group, somehow they were now more entrenched.

My intention was to educate and inform so that the students, themselves, chose to alter their behaviour because they could see the benefits of change. Perhaps they might even become agents of change and model this behaviour to their peers – the first steps in a 'hearts and minds' approach. Undoubtedly, that session changed my view. I just wanted to enforce behaviour change by

> *rules and sanctions so that the boys had to behave differently. A tough approach – 'grab them by the balls, and their hearts and minds will follow'.*

Tough sanctions are appealing because working with values and attitudes is long term and difficult. Sometimes, it blows up in your face. Even so, in working with adolescent male behaviour, masculinity and sexuality, I knew there had to be a better way than laying down the law. Rules do have some effect, if enforced, but tend to leave underlying attitudes untouched. The antidiscrimination laws, for example, do not directly affect the values behind sexist and racist behaviour. Such things go underground – become more subtle – but don't go away just because laws are passed.

Since that class I have run many sessions, and no matter how skilfully I present issues I am still struck by the range of boys' reactions to this topic. There always seem to be some boys who don't get the message, who are switched off, who couldn't care less or who cannot see the relevance to them. Most boys listened but a number were just going through the motions. A few were concerned and wanted something to be done about it.

A framework for working with attitudes

The most useful way I have found to understand these reactions is to view the range of individual and group reactions as forming a continuum of resistance. This continuum covers a range of behaviours, from a refusal to believe that the issue exists at all to a willing engagement with the problem. At one end there are those boys who entirely reject the issue and do not recognise that it arises. It is therefore not a problem. (For example, they may be engaging in low-level sexual harassment and consider their behaviour as perfectly normal.) At the other end of the continuum are those who actively seek resolution of the problem.

The five positions along the continuum are as follows – using the example of a teacher trying to work with boys to address harassing and playground violence.

1. Denial

Here the boy cannot see that there is anything wrong with harassing others. There is no violence occurring – 'What's wrong with you, anyway?' There is no availability for any learning on this topic, and the boy cannot see the relevance of what the teacher is going on about. This student either writes the teacher off and mentally leaves or gets into a heated argument.

2. Trivialisation

In this position the boy does realise what is happening – 'So what?' 'That scuffle last week, well Jonesy had it coming, didn't he? What's a bit of blood anyway?'. Then there is a quick change of subject, jokes and a diversion to other more 'significant' events. There is some room for learning but not much.

This student is likely to stir others or use the group attention to provoke something in the classroom.

3. Powerlessness

Students here do see this kind of violence in the playground and don't like it much, especially when it happens to them. They are compliant, may be apathetic or confused and go along with the group. When asked their opinions they often 'don't know'. When pushed they will find someone else who is responsible or is to blame. Their availability for learning is reasonable but they are unlikely to put anything into practice. These students can stay lazy and uninvolved as long as they do the minimum the teacher requires.

4. Coming to terms/Identity

In this position the students are aware of the problem and are interested in change. The key thing here is how their relationships with the group will be affected if they were to take a stand. The question is, 'What will it mean for me if I do speak out against harassment?' Their availability to learning is reasonably high and they are ready to learn skills.

5. *Action*

Students in this position want others to be involved and together they will take action. They are sick of the constant abuse and violence and want to do something about it. They will put information and skills into use and have a high availability for learning. They are likely to see the boys at *Level 1 – Denial* as a bunch of idiots, and in return they are despised by that group as teachers pets or 'brown-noses'.

Levels of resistance	*Key messages*
1. Denial	It doesn't happen.
	It doesn't affect me.
2. Trivialisation	It happens but it doesn't matter.
	It doesn't affect me.
	I have no responsibility.
3. Powerlessness	It happens and it affects me.
	It's not my fault. It's someone else's responsibility.
	What difference can one person make anyway?
4. Coming to terms/ Identity	It happens and it affects me.
	I have some responsibility.
	What does it mean for me if I get involved?
5. Action	It exists, I'm involved, I want to do something.
	How can I help?

This framework can be applied to any social issue. There is no position for someone to opt out. This is critical in topics related to masculinity and gender relations because we are all involved no matter how much we ignore the issue.

The aim in conducting programs that deal with attitudes and values is to get boys to move along the continuum towards action. It is, of course, possible to go backwards down the scale or get stuck. The continuum also provides a basis for evaluating where students are and how they move as a result of a program.

Students in the same position will have different reasons for being there. You may even see victims and perpetrators at the same end of the spectrum. A boy who provoked someone into bullying him may see this bullying behaviour as quite acceptable and would therefore be at *Denial*.

It is obviously much easier to teach students who are already at *Level 4 – Identity* or above. They are ready to put skills into practice and take action. Similarly, it is pointless trying to teach relationship skills to boys who are obsessed with scoring points off others.

By far the most difficult groups are those stuck at *Denial* and *Level 2 – Trivialisation*. These two positions are attractive to boys interested in power. Denying and trivialising constitute rejections of the need to relate to someone else's point of view and are typically regarded by boys as powerful. I see the major work in changing boys' attitudes is in creating an opening in the culture of *Denial* and *Trivialisation* so that change is possible. The task here is mainly revealing the need for change.

Critically, this framework generates clear implications for program success or failure in terms of whether we are teaching for skills, knowledge or attitudes. In teaching about masculinity it is essential to recognise boys' levels of openness to learning on this topic. Someone in *Denial* is basically not available for new information on that issue. It is pointless teaching skills or knowledge if they can't see the relevance. Similarly, someone in *Trivialisation* will find endless jokes and distractions to undermine what you are trying to get across. At this end of the continuum it is necessary to teach for attitudes.

At *Level 3 – Powerlessness* you can teach for knowledge. Boys will take in information but won't usually put it to use. They are resistant to learning skills. At *Level 4 – Coming to terms/Identity* boys are interested and ready to learn more. Someone at *Level 5 – Action* is already onside and wants to know how to be more effective. These students are ready for skills. In most classes the boys will spread across the continuum. I have found that if I can work effectively with attitudes and values then the level of resistance is reduced.

Often schools focus exclusively on one area, such as skills or knowledge, and are disappointed that the students don't take in and use what they were supposed to learn. Teaching skills against resistance is also hard work, so the natural tendency as busy teachers would be to teach information. For example, in a

Personal Development class dealing with emotions, it is a lot easier to list and categorise twenty different emotions than to work with boys' emotional expression and discomfort – or even to name the emotions that they experience regularly.

What then are effective strategies for working with attitudes at the *Denial* and *Trivialisation* levels of resistance?

Effective strategies

The most effective strategies are those that address the messages on which the positions of *Denial* and *Trivialisation* are based:

- 'It doesn't happen';
- 'It doesn't matter if it does'; and
- 'It doesn't affect me'.

Many boys have learned in a thousand different ways that the world favours the tough. Consequently learning will only occur once we get through this tough exterior, whether it is real or just a pretence. In my experience, information on its own very rarely works.

Because we all learn best from what we face in our own lives, any strategies that are experiential or evoke someone else's direct experience can be very effective. I try and work with small groups of boys so that there is sufficient safety to use activities such as drama, and action methods such as role-reversal. Often I will get the boys themselves to tell their story 'from the frontline'.

If students cannot experience something for themselves then the next best thing is to hear from someone who has. In this way, the fact that people from the 'real world' come in and tell their stories can be very powerful. No-one can deny their experience. The learning is in the story itself, particularly when it contains the personal and deeply felt issues of the guest. The students cannot help but be affected by, for example, the emotional life of an ex-bikie or soldier. They thereby experience a personal link to the effects of intimidation and threats of violence.

I also use activities that provoke a sense of dissonance in boys. This is a feeling of unease or discomfort when we become aware that *what we do* does not match *what we say we do*. Dissonance is quite a powerful motivator. When it occurs in relation to personal behaviour there is a 'teachable moment' where previously resistant students take in key information and learn something new.

The message behind the behaviour

I developed this approach after several boys-only group discussions on relationship issues fell somewhat flat. I wanted to get at the values behind the boys' behaviour and the way they explained that behaviour to themselves. I wanted boys to see the need for change in the way they thought about being male.

> *The first step is for the boys to brainstorm. I ask them to list the things they value in their peers and those they find difficult and would like to change: 'What do you really like about the way your mates behave?' and 'What really gets you about the way your mates sometimes behave?'.*

Looking at these two lists, we discover that many of the things boys value are also linked to those they'd like to change. For example, someone's sense of humour may be valued but not the put-downs that come with it.

The list of behaviours that boys want to change varies from group to group. They might want to do away with such things as: big-noting themselves, putting others down, 'dropping you' suddenly, stealing, crying and talking behind your back.

> *Choosing from the boys' list of things to change, I ask each boy to recall a specific incident where he was present. The next step is to examine that incident for the messages that the person displaying the behaviour is giving about himself. This is the crucial, reflective stage of the exercise – it asks participants to think in a different way about behaviour. Instead of seeing behaviour directed outwardly in reaction to others (e.g., 'You made me') this strategy focuses on what the speaker's words and actions reveal about himself and his values.*

> *When the key behaviour is acted out I can focus the boys' attention on the main character and the messages in his behaviour. For example, 'If Jim walks in and says something to put you down, what is he saying about himself? Let's do it and see.'*

> *Working out the message can be tricky, The way the message is phrased can cause difficulties of interpretation. This can make or break the strategy. It may take a while to come up with the actual message which the person is giving about themselves. Usually boys come up with 'you' statements. For example, 'You're an idiot', which I convert into a 'values' statement, 'I'm more*

important than you'. One way to maintain the focus on values is to get students to complete sentence stems such as:

> *Being successful as a male means . . .*
> *Touching means . . .*
> *Power equals . . .*
> *Men are only valued when . . .*
> *Expressing feelings is . . .*
> *Being a woman means . . .*

The aim is to compile a list of simple phrases or slogans – our value statements – with which we can then all agree or disagree. By the end of the strategy the boys will make a judgement about each statement in terms of whether it applies to themselves: 'Is this something you believe to be true? Is this something you live by?'.

It is important to work through this process, using examples, before asking the boys to break into small groups to create their own value statements and list the messages they see in each. Usually I ask each group to choose two examples to work through from the original list of behaviours that we want to change. After ten minutes or so they present the messages they see are presented to the rest of the group. I might use only some of their messages or rephrase them into more 'useable' value statements.

Common messages behind some boys' behaviours

Fighting (aggressor)
I'm better than you.
I'm more important than you.
Your feelings don't count.
My image is more important than my physical safety.
Talk is weak.
Power equals dominating others.
Being stronger makes you right.

Put-downs
I'm better than you.
It's not OK to make mistakes.
Power means making you look or feel stupid.

My image is more important than your feelings.
Your feelings don't count.
Being different is not acceptable.

Posing/Big-noting

Getting attention is more important than my relationships.
My image is more important than the truth.
It's not safe to be myself.
Being accepted is more important than who I am.
I am not acceptable as I really am.

Spitting

Power means forcing you to take notice of me.
Power means doing what I want no matter how it affects you.
I'm more important than you.
Being a man means not caring what others think.
Being a man means you don't control me.

> It can be very effective to draw from the actual behaviour and comments as they occur in the classroom. In one session an outspoken teenage boy began arguing the point about prostitutes at Kings Cross. After a bit of clarification we had the following exchange:
>
> 'They're sluts, right? That's why they're doing it.'
>
> 'The point isn't what you think they are or why you think they're doing it. They might be doing it for a whole range of reasons that we don't know about. The point is: "What does that say about you? What message are you giving about yourself by having to see them as sluts?"'

Then came one of those moments of silence. The pieces visibly fell into place as the boy began applying all the usual put-down messages to his own behaviour. ('I'm better than you', 'Your feelings don't count', 'My image is more important than seeing you as a human being'.) The boy went quiet and remained thoughtful for the rest of the session. He had obviously never thought about his behaviour in this way before.

Real-life values

Having established our list of messages the next step is to apply them in our lives. I might introduce this by saying something like: 'These are the things we don't like in our mates and other boys' behaviour, but in fact we all behave like this from time to time. When we behave like this these are some of the messages we are giving about ourselves. Let's consider these statements from our own experiences and perspectives. Are these the values we believe in ourselves? Do you agree with these statements?'.

Using the list of messages, I get the boys to vote on each value statement indicating whether they agree, disagree or are unsure. In values voting, participants physically indicate their opinions – for example, by raising their hands (agree), folding their arms (unsure) or dropping their hands towards the floor (disagree). It is a simple yet effective way of getting a quick response without having to go through explanations. It is very useful with reticent or shy groups.

Once the group has voted I extend discussion by using a range of questions such as: 'Is this something you believe about yourself?', 'Is this belief going to help you in your relationships?'. In relation to slogans such as 'Power equals strength' or 'Talk is weak', I would ask, 'Can you think of anyone who is powerful without being strong?'. (Some responses have been Fred Hollows, Mother Theresa, Kerry Packer, Carmen Lawrence and, for some, their mum.) Other questions might be, 'What other ways are there of being powerful?' or 'When is talking really powerful rather than weak?'. Essentially I am challenging the value statements listed.

By the time we have been through the list, the group finds that we have disagreed with a majority (sixty-five to ninety-five percent) of these statements. In pointing this out to the group I might ask various questions: 'Why do you think we behave in ways that give messages we don't actually agree with? Doesn't this suggest we act in ways that are not the real "us" – that there is a lot of pretending involved in being male? Is that true? Is that your experience? Does everybody have to put on an act? What is so important to us that we have to put on an act for it? How does it feel to know you aren't being honest about who you are – that nobody is being honest about who they are?'.

The boys nod and smile as everyone realises they are playing the same game of pretence. Now the group is aware of the dissonance that goes along with projecting an image of masculinity.

Moving towards change

This exercise aims to encourage an open and honest discussion about being male and what it means for each of us. In particular I raise the issue of how feelings are denied and ignored by boys because feelings are seen as a sign of weakness. The first step towards change is realising that there are choices: boys often accept stereotyped male behaviours as being the right way for them to act without realising that there are other options. By recognising that there is a choice, it is possible to consider what we really do want in our relationships and how we might behave in order to get our needs met.

Adolescent boys often have difficulty in expressing feelings, especially the softer and more vulnerable (i.e., 'feminine') feelings. Yet, when asked, girls in the relevant peer groups will say that the ability to express feelings is a quality they prize in boys. It seems to be part of personal skills such as being aware of your needs and valuing honesty and trust in relationships.

Even young males see themselves as having to live up to 'being a man'. Most will be aware of the discomfort of pretending to be one thing while they suppress any thoughts and feelings to the contrary. They create (for the outside world) an 'acceptable' male image for themselves. Many boys derive almost all their male identity from this image and place little or no importance on their inner experiences as males. They then pretend that this image they present to the outside world *is* in fact who they are.

It is possible with groups of boys to open up a discussion that allows them to be relatively honest about their lives and what they want for themselves. Many boys tell me that they had never talked in this way before. Some find it a relief to be able to relate to other boys without all the 'bullshit' screens.

> *Our discussions soon lead the group to accept that we all project a superficial image, that we are all much more than that, and that we are interested in developing relationships beyond the superficial level. The group is now ready to examine which changes it would like to see and how they might occur. In other words, they are ready for skills development.*

> *During this exercise, one group of Year 9 boys realised it was possible to drop their macho images and not be destroyed. They felt safe, probably because I was there backing up the ground*

rules we had agreed on. Following the realisation that everyone is in the same boat, the next question is always the key one.

I ask, 'Given that we often hide who we really are, what kind of relationships do you really want in your lives?'. This can be followed by a range of different questions: 'What do you mean by trust?', 'How many people can you really trust in your life now? ('None' is an acceptable answer)', 'Are the people we trust more likely to be male or female?' 'Why?'.

The questions focus mainly on what the boys would choose to have in their lives. The aim is to show them that they do control those choices. This encouragement supports the development of their self-reliance, enabling them to be more effective in their relationships.

The Year 9 boys said that they had never talked like this before. I realised that from this point it would be possible to move on to skills training. In fact they had already started by listening to each other.

Conclusion

The essence of my work with boys has been to find ways of addressing their resistance (to dealing with masculinity and their own behaviour) and to lead them to a new level of self-awareness. Working with boys and masculinity is personal, risky and can be exhausting. However its time has come. Many schools and teachers are grappling with the issues daily. We now need to take the next step and address concerns about boys and masculinity systematically across schools.

Rollo Browne consults to schools on boys' education, masculinity and gender relations. He presents regularly at conferences and staff development seminars. Rollo began teaching in Aboriginal communities in the Northern Territory more than fifteen years ago. Returning to New South Wales, he became an educator with the Family Planning Association, developing programs such as 'Year 10 Boys and Masculinity' and the Cleveland Street Antihomophobia Seminars. Subsequently he worked with the Human Rights Commission in the areas of privacy, race and sex discrimination. He now has his own company, conducting a variety of manager-development programs in organisations.

Boys and relationships

Can a program really change boys' attitudes and behaviour? *David Shores,* one of the developers of the Boys and Relationships Program in South Australia, believes this is only possible when the new values become an integral part of the school – which means being accepted and modelled by the teachers!

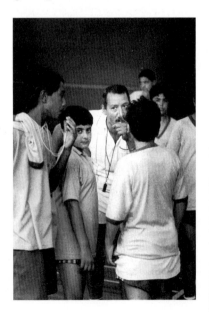

What to do with the boys?

A statement overheard in a staffroom recently went something like this.

The school's done Equal Opportunity and harassment stuff and the boys seem to be worse! They even use the knowledge and the vocabulary to blatantly harass others. They seem to have got better at it. It certainly hasn't stopped!

To me, this was of key relevance to the issue of how to influence boys' attitudes and behaviour. So what *can* we do with the boys?

The Boys and Relationships Program

We developed the Boys and Relationships Program as a preventive response to the large number of referrals of boys for aggressive and antisocial behaviour. The program aims to get boys to argue for their own change rather than telling them why they must change.

It was initially developed in 1990 as an activity-based program for boys in Years 5, 6 and 7, and has since been adapted to fit R-7. The content fits within the framework of the National Statements and Profiles in Health and Physical Education. It complements existing strategies that address sexual harassment, the needs of girls in education and protective behaviours. It is in the process of being adapted for junior secondary use.

The program aims to address the gender issues that:

- encourage antisocial behaviour and violence; and
- limit boys' behavioural, social and academic options.

The two themes

The program in no way sets out to blame male students. It uses two themes, firstly, to raise awareness of how elements of male conditioning often lead to destructive behaviour and, secondly, to explore options and alternatives to such behaviours and the structures that keep them in place.

The two themes are: 'Males Often Hurt Themselves and People They Love' (and we often add – 'When Things Don't Go Their Way'); and 'Things Are Changing'.

The program is set out as a series of eight activity-based lessons. Each lesson has a range of different exercises or approaches to particular topics. There is far more in each lesson than can comfortably be covered in the time, so it is up to teachers to select the aspects they see as relevant for their particular students.

The topics include: Changing Roles, Feelings, Expressing Feelings, Models of Behaviour, Looking at Heroes, and Conflict Resolution. At the beginning of each lesson a few minutes is spent discussing aspects of the two themes which run throughout all the lessons and tie the program together as a whole. Media articles, especially newspapers, are used to illustrate these themes.

The Shark Survival Game

Here's an example of how a lesson may develop.

Lesson 4 – Models of Behaviour (*Aggressive, Passive, Assertive – The Shark Survival Game*)

In this game, participants find themselves floating on life-rafts (PE mats) in shark-infested waters. They are faced with the fact that, progressively, their rafts are breaking up (the PE mats are taken away one by one over time) and the sharks are circling. At this point, whether they are conscious of it or not, the boys are choosing their responses from three possible behavioural options.

I win–you lose   *Aggressive*
I lose–you win   *Passive*
I win–you win   *Assertive*

As the game progresses, the teacher mentally notes the behaviour of the students and the consequences of that behaviour. This becomes the basis of a follow-up discussion, including teacher input on these three behavioural options.

For example, this may involve questions, such as: 'Which one did you choose?', 'What was the result from your point of view?', 'What was the result from the others point of view?', 'Was it a useful choice overall?', 'Can you imagine yourself choosing another option?'.

As you can imagine, the boys often choose the 'I win–you lose' option. Within the context of the game (and bearing safety in mind) it may well be a useful and exciting choice. Similarly, many boys choose the 'I win–you win' option and were extremely creative in keeping each other from the sharks' jaws. Some boys chose the option of getting eaten up rather than tackling the rafts.

At this stage the teacher points out that all three options can provide successful and useful choices if weighed up carefully. Unfortunately, many males are stuck with just one – the aggressive option!

Now the link can be made with the theme 'Males Often Hurt Themselves and the People They Love'. Appropriate newspaper articles can be used to illustrate the point in a nonjudgemental yet concerned manner. Examples abound of men who hurt themselves and others by using the aggressive option inappropriately. Examples that are used include sieges after evictions or retrenchments, violence towards (including murder of) wives or partners that choose to leave a relationship, self-destructive behaviour as a result of financial difficulties, and violence as a reaction to problems at school.

Each unit works in a similar fashion. There are activities and discussions in which boys offer their opinions and are prompted to examine their options and the consequences of their choices.

What do the boys say about the program?

We expect that the program will be useful for all the boys, not just the 'problems'. Many of the boys are quite interested in the sessions while others are not so forthcoming. Some typical responses in the written evaluations are as follows.

I liked:
- the shark game and the cycle and learning about it;
- learning about traps;
- Leonard getting tied up with traps but it was a shame that he didn't explode;
- sharks and the king is coming;
- I didn't like anything;
- how we all working together.

I didn't like:
- nothink;
- all the writing including this;
- anything much;
- how he asks what you feel.

I learned:
- about traps, how they are formed and what they do;
- how to notice when I was stewing and how to cool down;
- a few things;
- how to control your temper.

As a male I think:
- we are good but we should learn some methods of control;
- we should do more housework, and girls, females, should go to work;
- nothink;
- about sport;

How do we teach them?

Having established useful content of what to do with the boys, the next issue was, 'How do we teach them?'. Experience has shown that this can be difficult!

When we were introducing the idea of a group for boys, we received the following comment from a Year 6 boy: 'It's not fair! The boys always get the blame!'.

As a teacher with a background in Special Education and Child Protection (and someone who has been involved in running groups for 'Men who are troubled by their violence') I find the problem of determining how we teach the boys worrying, intriguing and challenging. In thinking about it, I return to my basic beliefs about learning, which have been practised and honed over a period of thirty years in education, especially in Special Education where we are often dealing with reluctant or noncooperative learners.

Eight principles

These beliefs can be condensed to eight key principles:

Principle 1
Find where they're at without putting them offside.

Principle 2
Teach them where they're at.

Principle 3
Affirm them for where they are at (and move them on).

> *We use newspaper articles to illustrate the program's two themes. For example, once when asking the boys to make sense of a reported murder–suicide, the conversation went something like this.*
>
> Student (with obvious resentment): *'She probably ran out on him so he went and fixed her up!'*
>
> Teacher (with some concern at the vehemence of the comment): *'Thanks for that, Angelo. That's certainly how many people would make sense of this article. Over the next few weeks we will be looking at other ways of interpreting this behaviour.'* (For example husbands, traditionally, literally owned their wives and children: things are changing!!)

Find, affirm and then teach them where they're at! It's not easy!

Principle 4
Don't blame the student if they fail to learn what I'm trying to teach them. Do I need to review my methods? How can I make it relevant for the student?

The bottom line is, what's in it for them to take on this new information or behaviour? What's in it for them *not* to take on this new information?

There are many approaches to this. Our approach focuses on the expanded options and flexibility for males that have the capacity to enrich their lives – especially in personal relations!

> *When expanding on our 'Things Are Changing' theme, we asked a group of boys if their fathers were at their births (an option not available when my sons were born).*
>
> *Greg piped up,'Yep, my dad was there. It was great. Do you want me to bring the video?'*

Principle 5

Find some area of connection with the student. How are we the same? Do I really understand how they see the world and see themselves in the world?

> *For example, we use carefully chosen self-disclosure (by the adults) to put ourselves in all of the models of anger, etc. The implication is that 'we get angry too'. We have a problem in our society around anger and I find this is a useful way of monitoring myself. Other teachers do, too: 'I use parts of what I learned at the day's training to monitor my own behaviour.'*

Principle 6

Learning is enhanced and integrated more effectively within a context of humour, activity and shared, valued individual experiences.

We stress listening to boys! This doesn't mean give them more time – they get more than their fair share already! By listening, we mean are we understanding (valuing) the way they see the world. This does not necessarily mean agreeing or dismissing their behaviour.

> *The following example involved a tired teacher on lunch duty dealing with an incident.*
>
> Irate student: *'I only hit him once. It didn't hurt! It's not fair! He took my lunch, he deserved it!'*
>
> Teacher (fed up, just wanting to have a break): *'I don't want to hear that rubbish. You need to take responsibility for your behaviour!'*

Principle 7

The more a learner feels safe (that is, unthreatened by the material or presenter) the more he is open to listening and considering new information. This may be enhanced if an element of choice is introduced.

> Student in boys' group, (angry, irate): *'This is a lot of crap! It's stupid!'*
>
> Teacher (interpreting his behaviour as threatened): *'If this is uncomfortable for you, Mark, it's fine with me if you go back to your seat and finish your Science project.'*
>
> *This not only 'takes the heat off' Mark (who will still be able to hear the information at his seat if he chooses), it informs the others that they too have some power in the situation – it's not being forced on them.*

Principle 8

How may I be unknowingly teaching the opposite to my stated objectives? As a Child Protection Adviser I was supporting a teacher implementing the Protective Behaviours Program in his class. We were introducing the theme, 'We all have the right to feel safe all the time'.

> Teacher: *'Well, girls and boys, this is our new theme.*
>
> Then (in an aside to a nonattending child): *'Rodney, come here and sit by me.'*
>
> Rodney (with a frown): *'Do I have to?'*
>
> Teacher (with indignation): *'Right now! And don't give me that look, young man!'*
>
> *Rodney moves, roughly pushing and disrupting others. Sits with a crash, knocking another pupil.*
>
> Teacher (quite annoyed): *'Right, that's it! Get out! I'll see you about this later.'*
>
> *Our aim was to teach the topic, 'We all have the right to feel safe all the time'. That aim was achieved for many of the students. However, Rodney may well have learnt – 'We all have the right to feel safe unless you annoy bigger people'.*

Working with boys on issues concerning the construction of masculinity is increasingly being seen as a useful (if not critical) next step in establishing gender equity.

Power, status and control

When planning the sessions to address boys' attitudes to relationships it quickly became apparent that the issues of power, status and control were paramount. Boys and men have traditionally defined themselves within these terms of reference. What is most interesting is that, similarly, power, status and control have been, and to a great extent still are, major considerations when evaluating teachers. It's important to remember that the overemphasis of power, status and control, in any relationship, interferes with good communication and interaction.

> Student (waiting at detention room door): *'Teachers are up themselves. They think they can do anything!'*

We as presenters began to realise the fuller implications for teachers of these issues concerning power, status and control. Participants told us how valuable it was for them. Consequently, our training sessions expanded from the initial half day (looking at the Boys and Relationships Program as it applied to boys) to a full-day session in which the adults had the opportunity of applying the principles to themselves.

The full-day workshop covered a wide range of issues including anger, aggression, beliefs about masculinity, alternative behavioural options, modelling and conflict resolution. Two important sections revolved around the issue of power. They were: i) helping teachers interact more effectively with boys by looking at themselves; and ii) models of power.

In over forty awareness-raising training days with teachers and parents, the emphasis shifted from a half-day session on content to full-day sessions. We now spend half a day on the process. Questions arise, such as: How do we teach it? How can we teach this content in a way that is most likely to be listened to by the boys, especially the resistant, aggressive and defensive ones?

Power, conflict and problem-solving techniques

Where do boys as young as five learn the 'power over' behaviours that we are trying to eradicate? I believe they learn from observing the behaviours, problem-solving techniques and power strategies they see in the world around them. This begins at home and most definitely continues in the school.

An incident at lunch time in the school yard, while we were discussing issues from a workshop.

School counsellor: *'This idea about modelling power and a range of conflict-resolution styles is really interesting. Excuse me a moment. Geoffrey, will you pick up that paper for me love?'*

Geoffrey (shaking his head): *'It's not my paper.'*

Counsellor (cajoling): *'Come on, Geoff. Come on, just pick it up.'*

Geoffrey, arms folded (more defiantly): *'It's not my paper!'*

Counsellor (irritated, possibly embarrassed by my presence): *'I'll ask you once more, then you are on a warning, Step 1. Pick up that paper, please!'*

Geoffrey (angrily snatching up the paper and throwing it into the bin): *'It's not fair. It's not my paper.'*

Counsellor (to me): *'That boy is such a hopeless case. He's so uncooperative and aggressive!'*

I'm including this anecdote as a useful example of a certain type of interaction, not to pass judgement on whether the counsellor was right or wrong. In terms of learning about nonaggressive conflict-resolution or power-sharing strategies, the lesson that was probably confirmed for Geoffrey was that people who have power can force others to do things. It doesn't mean that 'power over' is always bad, wrong or not often essential. Simply that if we use it all the time to solve our problems then our pupils will use it too!

Keeping our school grounds clean is important. How can we combine this with a lesson on social interaction that does not rely on 'power over' to achieve its ends? In many schools this is not a new idea – lots of interactive schemes are used. One principal I know picks up the papers that bother her, and many of her pupils choose to join in. This is just *one* way.

Such an example can be a minefield when working with teachers. They may choose to feel blamed, guilty, angry, insulted, devalued or patronised. All of these possibilities have one thing in common. None of them is likely to facilitate teachers in looking at or taking responsibility for their parts in the interaction, conflict or incident. It is really important to stress that we are not talking about 'goodies and baddies'. We are talking about creating an environment in which people feel sufficiently comfortable to look into themselves for insights and thereby begin to practise (and so model) the very things we are asking the boys to begin doing. Firstly they need to see, then take responsibility for their parts in any interactions.

Programs don't work

> Boys programs don't work. I tried it in Term 4 last year and it didn't make the slightest difference to the boys' behaviour. You can't make them do anything!

I agree absolutely with this comment from a frustrated and disgruntled school counsellor. If you think that you can significantly change the behaviour of boys (especially those resistant ones) through a series of eight lessons, then your experience of behaviour change is very different to mine.

Programs alone don't work. The values, concepts and language presented in a program need to become an integral part of the class and/or school. Once they are integrated, modelled personally (as well as professionally), valued and reinforced by the adults, then and only then is the climate ripe for attitudinal and behavioural change in the pupils.

Yes, you guessed it. Children learn from what you do as well as what you say! Programs on power sharing may begin to work if we as teachers reveal the people we really are: by talking about things that worry us, telling the students when we feel powerless or scared, dropping our powerful fronts and feeling safe enough to talk with them.

Looking for icebergs

> A wonderful example occurred in a school which was using the iceberg model of anger. In the program we use this model as an alternative to the traditional ways of making sense of aggressive behaviours, such as 'he just went off his head' or 'the teacher cracked a fruity', etc. It takes a view that anger is often a secondary emotion and covers a deeper, less acceptable one for individuals, especially males.

The class teacher used herself as an example of an iceberg in action. After a particularly stressful lunchtime (during which her relief for lunch duty was ten minutes late, her ordered lunch didn't arrive and the principal kept her talking till after the bell), she exploded at her class who were 'mucking around' in the line when she arrived. ('The teacher cracked a fruity.') By the end of the day (when she had calmed down) she chose to use what had happened to bring the iceberg model alive. It was a way of sharing her understanding of the experience with her class.

'Did anyone notice an iceberg at the door just after lunch?'

Pupil (with a smirk): *'Yes, it was you.'*

Teacher: *'That's right, you all saw a lot of anger at the top of the iceberg. What do you think was going on underneath?'*

Women working with boys' groups

This story also raises an interesting question. Is it OK, legitimate, politically correct, practical, safe or effective for a female teacher to work with groups of boys running a boys program? We believe that the very best leadership team is a woman and a man working together. Together they can model an equal partnership in action. In most schools the reality is that staffing doesn't allow such luxuries. Some schools overcome the problem by working collaboratively with outside assistance (such as staff from community health centres, etc.), especially with men who have a background in boys' and men's groups. However, as the majority of teachers are women (in primary and junior primary schools) our experience is that well over fifty percent of classes that attempt the program are run by female teachers. There are at least two reasons for this: i) male teachers don't exist in the school; and ii) the male teachers in the school feel unclear about the reasons for boys' groups (or feel threatened or blamed) and refuse to participate.

'Male teachers must take responsibility for the violence and harassment perpetrated by male students in schools' (This was a headline in a teachers journal.)

We agree that male teachers can and do exert enormous influence over boys' behaviour by the ways in which they act, resolve conflict and interact with others. The problem is, how do you get them to see this and begin to participate in running programs for boys?

We know from talking with women (and men) who have taken a strong interest in girls programs, it is not effective if it something that you use in your professional life only. It has to bring about profound changes in your personal life too. As we see when working with boys, men often find the thought of personal change extremely threatening.

However we have been pleased to observe a major shift in the gender balance of people requesting to do our one-day training days since 1990. Originally of the thirty participants, about ten percent would be male. Now in training days for junior primary or primary, fifty percent are males. We are also getting more and more requests from secondary schools – with the majority of participants being male. These male participants tell us are there because they have heard that it's 'good'. That is, males are not blamed, criticised or made out to be the 'baddies'. They are clearly responsible for their actions, yes, clearly part of the patriarchal system that traditionally entrenches power, yes, but not blamed! The results speak for themselves.

Returning to the question of women running groups for boys, we believe that the best person to run a program which challenges boys (and is possibly seen as threatening) is someone who has already built up a strong personal relationship with the students – the class teacher. Throughout the primary school years, this will most likely be a woman. How can this be effective?

> In our training days we use the report of the National Committee on Violence in Australia, 1990, to add some light to the issue. It states: 'The use of violence to achieve ends that are perceived as legitimate is a principle that is deeply embedded in Australian culture.' (p. 66)

If a female teacher feels comfortable with that quote and the realisation that we have a problem in our culture, then she will be able to talk with the boys in a way that avoids blaming an individual or a group. We believe strongly that this keeps the boys remaining open and more able to listen to the information being presented. This approach in no way shifts the onus of responsibility from males for their actions! The facts are clear.

> *One of the most striking aspects of violence in Australia is that the vast majority of those that commit acts of violence are males! (National Committee on Violence in Australia, 1990, p. 33)*

We believe that the theme 'Males Often Hurt Themselves and People They Love' addresses this issue clearly and unequivocally.

Working with teachers

Having participated in the training of over 1000 school staff we have developed strategies, language and a range of approaches that are most likely to create an open, receptive audience. The principles are similar to those we use in working with the boys.

1. Nonjudgemental language and attitudes

At the beginning of the workshop we stress that what they are about to hear is not the absolute answer, the right way or the only way to make sense of boys' behaviour. We present the information as perceptions based on experience. We expect that other people will have different perceptions about male behaviour and we are not attempting to establish one truth. If people find this information useful, then they are free to use it. If not, then that's fine too. Participants are asked to provide feedback if they perceive any of the presenters' language or attitudes to be blaming or judgemental. We accept the feedback and reflect on it. This reinforces the point that no-one is the expert. A useful point to ponder is, 'How am I affected by my gender-biased socialisation that I'm not yet aware of?'. (If we were brought up in this society we have been affected by it!)

2. Teach them where they are at

To do this we use a worksheet called 'The Best and Worst Thing About Being Male'. It is completed anonymously at the beginning of the day and shared at the end. It has a number of functions To provide a bit of fun; let them experience an exercise we do with the boys; give us an insight into how they see the issues; and get them to focus on the issues of masculinity.

Being male

Best thing   Stand up to wee. Good at picnics. Always has a mother to look after them.

Worst thing	Hairy bodies. Feelingless! Discouraged from showing caring.
Best thing	Nothing. Males are the most victimised group in our society.
Worst thing	Being disenfranchised by those groups that control society.
Best thing	Don't have to fake orgasms.
Worst thing	Can't fake orgasms.
Best thing	Having most structured institutions set up to meet your needs. Able to walk alone at night.
Worst thing	Having to be strong. Having few situations or skills to allow males to express how they really feel.
Best thing	I don't have to wear a top when swimming. Drive fast, die young.
Worst thing	I can't express my deeper feelings without being somewhat ostracised. Drive fast, die young!
Best thing	Physical strength and the advantages that this brings in a society that traditionally favours males (careers, laws, etc.). I acknowledge this is changing but we have a long way to go yet!
Worst thing	Having to always (?) be competitive.
Best thing	Being a partner, father. No periods.
Worst thing	Having to confront stereotypes, presumptions by both men and women. Shaving every day. Difficulty in going part-time in many 'male' jobs (e.g., in the building industry).
Best thing	Get lots of attention in families and schools.
Worst thing	Pressured to be good at sports. High percentage involved in crime/gaols. Expected to be the provider.

3. Choice, safety and comfort level

Because the content of the material can be challenging to some participants, considerations of safety and choice are critical. We always give a 'self-protection statement' early in the session. We point out that we will be touching on issues that may be sensitive for some and ask that participants 'look after themselves'. (We suggest some options.)

We give some statistics and point out that within any group of twenty to thirty people there will be some that (at present, and certainly in the past) have been touched by violence. Simple observations and statements about the important link between safety and comfort level and learning can be made.

We make it clear that participation in the activities is up to the individual. We watch and gently comment on the 'power-over' strategies of 'dobbing in' or pushing others forward, and use 'one-step' removed language where possible. For example, traditionally schools have used 'power-over' techniques to a great extent.

We often include in our 'getting to know you' exercise the discussion option of 'How come you are here today? Did you volunteer or were you tapped by the principal?'. We give permission for this to be aired nonjudgementally and offer the option of daydreaming, doodling or just drifting off. This can often reduce tension.

4. Power, power sharing, conflict and conflict resolution

In any group the exercising of power is something that happens moment by moment. It's useful to bring this to people's awareness by verbalising how you are experiencing it at that moment. Often the exercising of power is extremely subtle.

Some conclusions

Working with boys exploring the social construction of masculinity is a relatively new and fascinating area for teachers. It's exciting, personally challenging, downright difficult and exhausting.

Since its beginnings in 1990 we have come to some conclusions about how the Boys and Relationships Program fits into the picture.

- There is a great interest in schools in the social construction of masculinity and how educators may effect change. The program is a useful vehicle for many teachers to begin this exploration.
- A large percentage of teachers use aspects of the program to understand and discuss student behaviour.
- A large percentage of teachers use aspects of the program to monitor their own behaviour.
- A significant number of teachers use aspects of the program to improve the educational outcomes for girls as well as boys.
- Schools and teachers take up to a year after their initial training to implement the program in classes.

David Shores has been involved in education for thirty years, with a focus in Special Education and, more recently, in Boys' Education. He is a private consultant and trainer in behaviour and learning and works part time as a support teacher at Payneham Support Services, Department of Education and Children's Services, South Australia.

Looking to fathers

Richard Fletcher, a leading advocate for involving fathers in schools, describes new initiatives, such as the Fathers Against Rape groups, nontraditional roles for men in school life and special 'dads' events (just for fun).

One night in Newcastle

By the time we finally opened the meeting there were almost fifty fathers present. The air was electric. You could almost hear the men thinking as they looked around, 'Gee, so many fathers in one school room . . . to talk about our kids'. It was basically a room full of strangers. Few of the men knew each other, even though they all had children at the high school. We knew that prior to this meeting the biggest male roll-up ever was when four dads came to a working bee to put up the cricket nets.

The large audience made the three of us from the Fathers Against Rape group nervous. As a group of fathers formed to run workshops for boys about preventing rape, we had experience talking to boys in groups. And we knew that the teachers and the mothers of the boys approved. What we didn't know is how the workshops would be received by the fathers. That's why we had suggested to the school that they invite fathers to the school.

The principal gave an introduction, indicating his support for the group, and we had the floor. After a short account of our beginnings – the rape of a teenage girl we knew, and the development of the idea of fathers going into schools to talk to boys about rape – we got down to business. We picked three dads sitting near the front and 'volunteered' them to answer some questions in front of the group. They looked a bit sheepish but agreed to turn their chairs around to face the audience and try to answer. We asked them to introduce themselves, including how many kids they had at the school. Then we asked them to say what was good about being a dad, what was difficult and what they'd like to see changed.

The first dad started willingly enough – he was a bricklayer and a footy coach – with two boys and a girl. But he faltered on the question of what was good and we started perspiring as the rest of the room waited while he scratched his head and mumbled. Fortunately, though, he went on to speak from the heart about what was difficult and the atmosphere thawed noticeably.

What worried him was the realisation that he could no longer properly protect his kids. They were teenagers now and going out in groups or on their own. While he was with them he was confident enough. With some gusto he described the school dance where some 'hoodlums' from a nearby pub gate-crashed the dance and threatened the younger boys there. He and some other fathers threw the gatecrashers out and chased them off. But the physical impossibility of protecting all three of his teenagers – protecting them from other teenagers or other men – had recently dawned on him. He felt trapped into helplessness as a result.

The second man, a self-employed businessman, had a boy and a girl. He also spoke best about what was difficult as a father. For him, the long work hours he felt were necessary for his business kept him apart from the family at crucial times – like mealtimes. In particular, he noticed that whenever the kids had problems – even if he were at home – they would always go to their mother first. Then, if it was serious enough, he would get to hear of it. He also felt trapped. His business needed time and he was missing out on an important level of intimacy with his children.

From there the debate in the room took off and a host of different questions and opinions flew around the room. Why did schools mollycoddle the students? Why were boys not doing so well? What about unemployment? How could parents stop them smoking when they did it at school? What about drugs and what could parents do about the pressure to buy expensive brands of clothing like *Reebok* and *Quicksilver*? After an hour or so the focus returned to fathers and how the men present could become more involved in the school. But the only practical suggestion to come forward was for a committee to be formed. Some of the men groaned at this and a representative from the school council pointed out the duplication. At the end, no clear direction for further action had emerged.

Recruiting fathers

As a strategy for recruiting fathers to be involved in the school, this type of meeting is probably a poor model. It starts, if you like, at the 'hard end' of male issues – stopping rape and dealing with male violence. Nevertheless, there are some lessons here.

The fact that fifty fathers turned up to discuss their sons suggests that involving fathers in schools is not, as is often said, a hopeless task. It may not be easy, but if it can happen in a fairly mainstream Newcastle suburb, it can happen anywhere. Of course the invitation to the fathers was not to discuss just any old topic. These dads came to discuss boys. Because there has been so little examination of boys' issues over the last twenty years, many parents are still thinking it is only their boy who has difficulties. And because boys' problems are just now being recognised as problems, it is important to focus parents' aware-ness on what we do know about boys' issues. One way to do this is to send a letter asking questions like, 'Did you know that boys are three times more likely than girls to be in a special reading class?'. (A survey form with examples of these issues is included in the endnotes.) Once fathers identify the areas they most want to do something about, they can then be approached by the school to help figure out solutions.

This brings us to the second feature of the meeting with fathers: the wide range of concerns expressed. Since few fathers (male guardians) attend school functions, it has been assumed that most fathers have no thoughts on school issues, but at our meeting, the men were concerned about curriculum, discipline, behaviour, standards, excursions, job training, school policies, leadership and violence. The breadth and strength of these con-cerns left us floundering. When the fathers asked if we would continue to meet with them, we refused, partly because of work commitments but also because we didn't know what to do next. We were having trouble making sense of it all, let alone finding a clear direction for the group.

If these dads are any indication, just getting men into the school grounds might not be enough. Even if they want to be involved, as these men did, they might not know how to find a suitable role. Schools will have to ask, offer and negotiate with fathers to make sense of their concerns and discover the sorts of activities that fathers see as valid.

Jobs for dads?

The lack of male involvement in schools – apart from male teachers – became a crucial issue for our group, Fathers Against Rape. For over two and a half years we had presented a 'Stopping Rape' workshop to boys in high schools throughout the Newcastle region. The feedback from the boys and the schools was extremely positive, an effect, we thought, of three related factors: the groups were small, they were all male and they were led by 'ordinary' dads. For each group of fifteen boys we would have a male teacher present, usually as part of the group, and at least two fathers. This gave the workshop both safety and a nonclassroom atmosphere. Those of us running the groups did not rely on any authority other than being fathers (the fathers included labourers, tradesmen, ministers and businessmen).

Even though the workshops themselves were successful, we were unable to convince any but a few fathers from the schools where we worked to help run the program. Looking around the schools, we noticed that fathers were restricted in the things they could do. Official jobs, such as president of the P&C, were all right, but activities which were traditional 'women's work', such as helping in the canteen or covering books in the library, seemed taboo for men. We realised too that the fathers we were trying to recruit had no experience of schools seeking them out to work directly with students. After many fathers' meetings we decided that until schools started to see fathers as capable of interacting successfully with students, our group would have little chance of convincing fathers to be involved with something as intimidating as 'Stopping Rape' workshops.

'So should we get a househusband?'

The ground-breaking *NSW Government Inquiry into Boys Education 1994* had as its first recommendation:

> *Programs should be developed to involve all parents, and fathers in particular, as active participants in their children's education.*

The report also said:

> *Boys particularly look to their fathers as their most important role model. Showing their children that they value non-traditional pursuits such as reading, music and the arts is a primary responsibility of fathers who want their boys to have a full and satisfying experience of life.*

There are two important points here. In the first place, while it is right to declare that fathers have a responsibility to their sons, simply pointing out this idea is unlikely to achieve much. Dads need to be offered a variety of 'active participation' roles in their children's education. This will take some creative thinking on the part of schools, and some courage to try new things on the part of the fathers.

The second important point is that fathers are already role models. When school staff discuss 'what to do about the boys', often the first strategy suggested is to have better role models for the boys. This is not surprising. Schools have used role models before. Women who are successful in business or engineering or who are apprentice electricians, for example, have been invited to address schoolgirls to show them that 'real' women were not all hairdressers or sales assistants. Schoolteachers are also very aware of the influence that pop stars or sports heroes have on the boys.

But there is a catch here. What worked for girls will not necessarily work for boys. The girls strategy had two aims really, one was to show that girls can do any job, but another was to urge girls to lift their sights. Teachers wanted girls to consider going into jobs traditionally thought of as male, and not just take any job, but a technical, well-paid, job. Quite sensibly, no-one suggested that girls get a job at the coke ovens in the steelworks! Instead they went for trades, business and technical jobs with good pay and conditions. For boys, as a group, the notion that they should lift their sights to business and technical careers doesn't make sense. Of course many boys will have jobs with poor pay and conditions, but overall, compared to girls, the boys will be ahead. For boys, the issue is not so much lifting their sights but broadening their horizons. Consequently, the high flyer approach to role modelling for boys is quite limited.

Who then are the good role models for boys? Teachers ask, 'So should we get a househusband to come and tell the boys how great it is to be home with the kids?' By their tone you know that this is not a serious question. They know that a househusband is not a 'star' in boys' terms. Some schools try to get both – the attractiveness of a 'star' and someone with the right values – by having a first-grade footballer in to talk about how he really loves to spend time with his kids. But this is a hoax. While the sports star may be sincere in his values, he is still a super competitive athlete and so the message which he reinforces is that winning is important, and performance, in sport or work (and of course for top sportsmen it is their work), is what counts.

Schools searching for big-name public figures to speak to boys are overlooking the interest boys (and girls) have in relating to respectful male adults. Even though it will take some work on the part of the school to break down the notion of 'women's jobs' in schools, recruiting fathers to become volunteers will provide an abundance of role models. The father selling drinks in the school canteen, the grandfather who listens to young children read and the uncle helping run the craft room are offering the students a much broader picture of men than a talk by a superstar can. This applies to all the pupils of course, not just the boys.

Naturally, having some students' fathers come to the school will not solve the difficulties of those without fathers. But why should these students not enjoy the contact with adult males even if they are not their own fathers? Most of the time that parents spend around schools they will be interacting with lots of children, not just their own. And we shouldn't be too stuck on biological fathers here, either. Invitations can be made to other males from the community to be part of the students' picture of what men can do.

For some schools, inviting fathers in will not be a new idea. But because it is a difficult area and overlooked as an important aspect of students' welfare, we rarely hear about any successes. I came across this example quite by accident at a Boys' Education seminar for teachers specialising in students with learning difficulties (ninety percent are boys).

Fathers' night

The invitation card featured a gorilla, an image chosen by the children as likely to appeal to their dads. '5/6 R are having a fun night to celebrate Father's Day', it said. It was sent out to the fathers (and male guardians) of Year 6 students. To the surprise of the teacher, nineteen dads turned up.

After the introductions, the first game was played – team hockey. Each father was teamed up with his own child. This went surprisingly well. Next came the presentations. Students read poems that they had written to their dads – appreciative, sometimes ambiguous, funny poems. Here is one:

My Dad

My dad is away on business a lot, and I don't get to see him very much.
He works very hard.
My dad gets to ride in planes nearly every week!
That lucky!
My dad sometimes says he would rather have two boys, but I know he doesn't mean it.
Sometimes we tease him.
He gets angry but he's really laughing inside.
We try not to get him cross, but, let's face it, we kids have to have SOME fun!
When he's sick we nurse him back to health – only for career practice though.
My dad's the one in our family who gives in to our pleadings.
To conclude this statement, if I wanted a slave, I would have my dad!

Katie

In the 'Guess Who' game each dad had a cardboard hat with the name of a celebrity written on it. (The dads couldn't see their name and had to ask questions to discover who they were.) During the preparation for this game, one boy told the class how his dad really thought that he (the dad) looked like Sylvester Stallone of 'Rambo' fame. So, on the night, they gave his dad the Sylvester Stallone hat. When the dad's questions led him to guess the answer, he burst into laughter, joined by the whole class.

Another hit was Katie's mother. Because her husband was away working, and wanting her daughter to be able to present her poem, Katie's mum dressed up in a suit and tie and came as Katie's father. Between the games and presentation the students served their dads supper as a sign of appreciation. At the end of the night the dads wanted to stay to play 'just one more' hockey match.

What is remarkable about this approach to dads is the absence of the work ethic. Instead of asking dads in to the school to help build a fence, or be on the P&C or even work in the canteen, this invitation was to a celebration. The men even played with the children! Feedback to the teacher from the mothers after the event included improved relations between the children and their fathers (or stepfathers) and a new interest in the children's school work by the men.

The future

It is important that schools across Australia take up the challenge of inviting fathers to share the work of schools and the enjoyment of interacting with young people. Because there are no experts in this area, there will be a great opportunity to learn from each other's experiences. Keeping in touch and sharing new developments can provide encouragement for us to follow-up the one-night stands used to get fathers through the gate. What are we waiting for? Let's do it!

Richard Fletcher taught Science in coeducational and all-boy high schools in Australia and overseas. In his subsequent work with the Health Promotion Unit in Newcastle, he pioneered the development of Men's Health and Boys' Health as areas of study. In 1992 he founded a community-based group, Fathers Against Rape, which conducted 'Stopping Rape' workshops with teenage boys in schools. He is a nationally recognised spokesperson on male health issues. As a lecturer in Health Studies in the Discipline of Paediatrics, University of Newcastle, he teaches Male Health Studies to nurses, trainee teachers, occupational therapists and medical students.

It's not the way guys think!

Wayne Martino, an English teacher in Perth, describes how a teacher provides an important model of masculinity for the students – and relates how he used a powerful father–son story to encourage boys to challenge their accepted views of masculinity and relationships.

The phone rings. It is a former colleague from school who wants to discuss her nephew's tertiary entrance results with me. He performed extremely well in Maths, Chemistry and Physics but failed English, achieving a score of thirty-nine percent.

She is ringing on behalf of his mother who is worried that this will affect his entry into university. She needs some advice about what options are available to a student who is in this situation. Despite the fact that he has achieved a high tertiary-entrance score, one university has indicated that he does not qualify for entry because he has failed to meet the literacy requirements – he has not passed English! Another university stipulates that students who fail English must sit for a special literacy test.

As I listen to the concerned voice on the other end of the phone, I can only think that this is a fairly representative situation for many boys. They do not value studying English and therefore do not feel motivated to learn in this subject. This, I intend to argue, is related to issues of masculinity and is the price that some boys must pay for adopting rigidly defined masculine codes of behaviour which influence the way they think and feel about studying English.

This, of course, has implications for all boys – not only in terms of their achievement in English, but also in terms of their development of important and necessary human capacities which have traditionally been associated with girls. It is important for boys to develop the capacity to express their emotions and to care for others.

I'd rather play footy!

In the course of my day-to-day teaching and in my interaction with students outside of class, I became acutely aware of differences in the behaviour, responses and attitudes of girls and boys. The girls tended to sit around quietly in groups chatting while the boys were out on the oval kicking the football or playing basketball. The boys tended to be more disruptive in class but also tended to answer more questions than girls.

I also noticed that, in English, the boys responded differently to the girls, often claiming that they found the subject boring and uninteresting. The boys tended to lose interest quickly and this was sometimes manifested in their tendency to disrupt the class and to draw attention to themselves.

In an attempt to understand these apparent differences I devised a survey which included the following questions and distributed it to 156 Year 10 students and to 93 Year 11 students;

1. Do you think English is a subject suited to
   (i)   boys
   (ii)   girls
   (iii)   neither sex
   (iv)   both sexes
   Give reasons for your answer.

2. Do you think that the texts you read/study are suited to
   (i)   boys
   (ii)   girls
   (iii)   neither sex
   (iv)   both sexes
   Give reasons for your answer.

3. Extended Response: What are your impressions of English as a subject that you are required to study at school? What do

you really think about English? Please feel free to make any comment that clearly expresses the way you fell about studying and participating in this subject.

4. Do you feel motivated to learn/study English? Give reasons for your answer.

The survey clearly indicated that there were differences in the way that boys and girls perceived English with the boys expressing their dislike for a subject which they considered to be feminine.

> *I believe this that English is suited to girls because most of the work is about emotions and feelings and girls are more used to this or have better practice at expressing their feelings.* (Steve)

> *English is more suited to girls because girls express their feelings . . . the texts are all about feelings and they're never action or interesting. I think English is boring and we know how to talk so why do we have to learn more? Also reading is lame, sitting down looking at words is pathetic. Watching TV and playing sport and the computer is way more interesting.* (Andrew)

The hard part – expressing feelings

These boys clearly see English as a subject which is more suited to girls because they see it as requiring students to express their emotions. Many of the boys' comments in class about English being boring and a waste of time have at their basis, I believe, this idea that English is more for the girls.

Perhaps boys' resistance to reading is also based on this premise that reading is for girls, as is indicated by Andrew's response. In fact, many of the boys tend to view English as being in opposition to other activities which they either enjoy or to which they feel they are more suited.

> *Boys don't read as much as girls because of sport.* (Michael)

> *I'm not sure about anyone else, but I would rather play footy.* (Scot)

> *I say this stereotypically that English is more suited to girls because boys don't read as much because of sport etc.* (Ben)

Sport clearly confirms these boys' developing sense of what it means to be a man. Through sport boys define themselves as *active* as opposed to *passive*, *strong* as opposed to *weak*, *tough* as opposed to *vulnerable*. It is within such a social context that these boys tend to identify English as a soft option not suited to them as males, since it does not really deal with the *heavy stuff*.

> *English is more suited to girls because boys like sport, heavy stuff but girls' personalities are more suited to English because they are usually more on the quiet side than boys . . . I don't actually like the texts I study this year because my personality doesn't fit the stuff I'm studying.* (Joshua)

Other boys define English as being in opposition to other subjects which they clearly value and perceive as more masculine.

> *I find English hard. It's because there are no set rules for reading texts. It's hard for me to express myself on paper and, therefore, I don't do as well as I do in other subjects.* English isn't like Maths where you have rules on how to do things and where there are right and wrong answers. [My emphasis] *In English you have to write what you feel and that's what I don't like.* (Shaun)

> *English to me is one of those subjects where it has its ups and downs. Most of the things we do in English are interesting but some get lengthy and make you want to fall asleep, e.g. the study of* Romeo and Juliet. *Also it gets a bit confusing at times because there are no real answers to things. The answer could be a variety of things, you're never really wrong.* It's not like Maths or Science where there is one set answer to everything. [My emphasis] (Leon)

Shaun identifies English as a subject which requires him to express his feelings and he finds this difficult. The reason for this could be explained perhaps in terms of the way in which he has been trained or taught to think, behave, act and respond as a male. It is in this sense, I think, that he perceives the learning tasks associated with English as somehow feminine and therefore inappropriate for him as a male. Furthermore, it is precisely this idea of English as a feminine subject that leads both these boys to define it as being in opposition to Maths or Science with which they clearly feel more comfortable. In Maths, unlike English, there are clear right and wrong answers!

I remember a boy commenting to me in class that he thought English was a Mickey Mouse subject. When I asked him to explain, he said that he didn't feel that we often dealt with facts or knowledge. According to him, it was more 'the airy-fairy kind of stuff to do with people's opinions, feelings and emotions'.

While the boys tend to reject English and to value Maths and Science, the reverse is true for girls. They tend to value English at the expense of Maths and Science. The girls appear to enjoy the freedoms that English allows – in terms of being allowed to express their feelings and in not feeling forced to follow strict guidelines or formulas in order to arrive at a definitive answer.

I feel motivated to study in English because it's a fun subject and you have freedom in English – unlike subjects such as Maths and Science – and your view isn't necessarily wrong. There is no definite right or wrong answer and you have the freedom to say what you feel is right, without it being rejected as a wrong answer. (Rochelle)

English is a very worthwhile subject because it is different to subjects like Maths which is all numbers and working out things. (Sarah)

Actually I really enjoy this subject very much . . . I think English is the easiest subject for me because for example in Maths, Science you have to know all the formulas etc. where English you only need to read and answer questions, essays etc. and I enjoy doing it . . . (Kate)

What all this points to, as I see it, is that English is perceived as requiring specific capacities which boys consider to be more suited to girls and which conflict with their views of masculinity. As one low-achieving Year 10 boy commented:

I don't like English . . . it's not the way guys think . . . This subject is the biggest load of utter bullshit I have ever done. Therefore, I don't particularly like this subject. I hope you aren't offended by this, but most guys who like English are faggots. (Brad)

What is particularly interesting is how this boy questions the masculinity of those boys who enjoy English and views them as homosexual. Moreover, he suggests that they are effeminate in some way for responding positively to a girls subject. This raises issues about how boys in their peer groups might police masculinity. Perhaps they do this through a series of put-downs directed at throwing into question a boy's sexuality. In any case, this boy rejects English as a worthwhile subject because of its association with femininity and feminine ways of knowing.

The above comments highlight the effects of a particular, dominant perception of masculinity. They demonstrate how such versions of masculinity influence patterns of learning and motivation for boys within the subject of English. Also, they point to the everyday effects of masculinity on boys' social and peer-group relations. This is reflected in the ways in which boys relate to one another within the context of their peer groups.

The social and emotional effects of masculinity

I first began teaching boys in 1992, having taught girls for six years. I became quite fond of my Year 9 English class but sometimes found it difficult to deal with the ways in which some boys tended to call other boys names – all in good fun. I recall one of the boys calling another boy 'boulder head' (or something to this effect), in jest, in the course of a small-group activity. I said that name-calling can sometimes hurt a person's feelings. The boy responded jovially: 'But, Mr Martino, he doesn't take offence. We always call each other names, it's just for fun!'

On one occasion I told them that I was concerned about the name-calling that I heard both inside and outside class and that I wanted them to be more aware of the feelings of others. I recounted an experience that I had had as a boy at school. I used to be called 'Big Ears' by my friends who thought that it was just a joke. It got to the stage, I told them, of not wanting to go to school anymore and of constantly looking in the mirror – trying to imagine and believe that my ears weren't really that big.

By relating to them an experience from my own life, I tried to get them to see the unintentional consequences of their name-calling – consequences which, perhaps, some of them had never considered.

> *Some weeks later I received a call from a mother of one of the boys, inviting me to dinner. Apparently her son, Craig, had spoken about me a lot at home. She wanted to talk to me about her concerns that he was not doing enough work and was just coasting along in English. I accepted the invitation and we arranged a time.*

During dinner Craig became subdued as his mother began tell-
ing me how very little work he was doing and how she believed
that a drop in his standard of work was related to this lack of
effort. She wanted to know how we could help him feel more
motivated in English. She made the point that he read avidly but
was not performing according to his ability.

I confirmed that he needed to do a lot more work in order to
achieve his potential. Craig started to cry quietly. After a couple
of minutes he was sobbing at the dinner table. This response sur-
prised me. I asked him if he felt really pressured at school. He
continued to cry, shaking his head.

When he eventually spoke he talked about how he could no longer
stand the names that he was being called at school by his friends.
He claimed that even though he was no longer called names in
class the practice persisted during recess and lunch, in the corri-
dors and on the oval. In fact, Craig had been at the centre of the
name-calling incident in my class that I described earlier.

We discussed possible ways of dealing with this situation, which
had – quite clearly – become unbearable for him. He definitely
did not want his parents contacting the school or the year
coordinator.

I suggested – as an initial measure – that I talk to the boys,
some of whom were in my English class. Craig was really concerned about drawing attention to himself and was afraid of the
consequences if his friends were to discover that he had actually
spoken about the problem.

The next day at school I spoke to the group of boys in my
English class who I knew were responsible for the name-calling.
I told them that I was still concerned about such teasing. They
claimed that they had stopped the name-calling but students in
other classes had persisted.

I stressed that they had to be more aware of how they were
making other students' lives miserable and that they needed to
make their other friends aware of this. These boys were receptive
and I could see that they really wanted to do something about
the situation.

Over time, the situation did get better and the name-calling
ceased. Craig began to feel more comfortable and relaxed at
school.

You might well ask, 'Well, what's this got to do with teaching boys English? What's the connection?'

I believe that my success as an English teacher is linked to the way that I relate to my students as people who deserve to be valued and treated with respect. Perhaps this is also connected with the fact that I am providing a different model of masculinity – especially in the way that a male English teacher can relate to students.

Discussing masculinity and gender stereotypes

The result of such experiences led me to consider the issue of addressing masculinity and gender in the English classroom. Clearly, if boys were rejecting particular ways of knowing as *feminine*, as a means of defining their masculinity, this needed to be addressed in the interests of both genders.

But how was I to target the construction of gender – and, in particular, masculinity – in a productive way? If boys were already feeling threatened about having to prove their masculinity (as was quite clearly the case), any attempt to focus on the issue of masculinity might lead them to be more resistant to change.

I decided to use a short story, 'The Altar of the Family' by Michael Wilding, to tackle this issue with my Year 11 English class. It is about a father who disapproves of his son playing with dolls and engaging in what he considers to be effeminate play with his younger sister. He even indicates one evening at the dinner table that he does not want his son, David, to turn into a 'lily-livered poofter'.

In order to live up to the expectations of his father, David eventually feels constrained to shoot a possum to prove his manhood.

'He was still with terror, the horror of shooting it convulsed his stomach, his bowel; he could already hear his sister's hysteria.'

This violent act leads him to feel sick. The text finally presents the reader with an image of boy who has been numbed by his experiences – who has been forced to repress his sensitivity and emotions in order to be accepted by his father. He is required to suppress these traits, which are considered feminine attributes and, in conflict with what is traditionally perceived to be appropriate manly behaviour.

At the end of the story the boy is described playing cricket, 'like an automaton figure on a mechanical clock, chiming futile time in the flat emptiness of eternity'.

The text appears to be encouraging readers to respond critically to the father and to the dominant model of masculinity he represents. Within this model a specific set of behaviours constitutes what it means to be a man: being tough; denying emotions and feelings; and engaging in particular manly practices and pursuits, such as hunting and playing sport.

It is in this sense that the text can be read as inviting a sympathetic reading of David, who is constructed as a victim of an oppressive set of gender expectations. In fact, this short story can be read as an example of the ways in which certain kinds of behaviours for boys are policed or controlled. It is in the sense that I thought it would be useful for exploring the specific effects of dominant models of masculinity.

After students had read the story in class, they were asked to complete the following activity.

The father

Below is a list of words that might be used to describe Mr Murray:

snobbish	*prejudiced*	*heartless*	*caring*	*impatient*
proud	*humorous*	*stupid*	*honest*	*dishonest*
ironic	*insecure*	*loyal*	*principled*	*traditional*
brace	*strong*	*honourable*	*insensitive*	*tough*
brutal	*intimidating*	*strict*	*manly*	*affectionate*
pragmatic	*sensible*	*self-controlled*	*religious*	*homophobic*

- *On your own, decide which of the words you would use to describe Mr Murray. Write them down. Add your own words to the list if you wish.*

- *Compare your list of adjectives with those of others in your group. Discuss any differences there may be, arguing for or against the inclusion or exclusion of specific words.*

- *Compile a list for your group to present to the class. If you cannot come to a consensus, present more than one list, explaining your differences.*

> • *Try to negotiate a composite list or lists on the blackboard,*
> *made up of suggestions from all groups. These lists should*
> *summarise possible readings of Mr Murray. Add words to*
> *your list to support your reading of the character.*

Interestingly, most of the students – boys and girls – chose words
which signalled their rejection of the father. They chose words
such as 'brutal', 'heartless' and 'insensitive' to describe the father
rather than more positive terms.

While the students chose very damning words to describe the
father, the opposite applied to David. I used the following activity
as a means of gauging the students' response to David.

The son

> *Although third person omniscient narration is used, it is David's*
> *thoughts and feelings that the reader is given access to.*
>
> • *Write your own list of words describing David.*
>
> • *Share your words with group members, and compile a list or*
> *lists to present to the class. Again, if you cannot agree, pres-*
> *ent more than one list, explaining your differences.*
>
> • *As a class, compare lists of words compiled by different*
> *groups. How do readings of David differ, and for what*
> *reasons?*

The boys tended to choose words such as 'caring', 'gentle', 'a
victim', 'lonely', 'quiet'. It was interesting that the boys, for the
most part, did not reject David as a wimp or question his
masculinity. They tended to see him as a victim and sympathised
with him accordingly.

I then asked the students to respond to the following question:

> *What do you think of David and the relationship that he has*
> *with his father? Write a response in which you outline what you*
> *think about these characters.*

The written responses from the boys further reinforced their
existing critical views of the father and their sympathetic views
of the son.

> *David's dad can only be described as an asshole. He leaves his*
> *wife to make a lot of the decisions about their children. David*
> *isn't allowed to play with the street kids and his dad objects to*
> *playing with his sister . . . Cricket is a fun game when you have*

> another 10 people playing it and to expect David to play cricket all day everyday must be a pretty sadistic demeaning activity . . . David's father was fighting with David's sister and she out-insulted him so the father had to make a cheap shot at David being a 'lily-livered poofter'. (Robert)

> My feelings toward David are mainly centred around pity and a desire to help him out of his ordeal. Help him, that is, if he were real which he is not. I find it hard to believe that David's father is so lame in his inexcusable excuses for being a complete idiot. The father's talk of manhood not only proves his idiocy, but illustrates his own self-consciousness in which he doesn't see himself as fully manly. (James)

It is interesting that Robert constructs the father as defensive in his verbal attack on his son while James raises questions concerning the father's insecurity about his own masculinity. The following response, in fact, reflects the extent to which the boys saw David as a vulnerable, sensitive boy who deserved the sympathy of the reader.

> To me David sounds like a gentle caring sort of person, whereas his father is the rough macho type of bloke. (Damian)

Other responses were also fairly representative of the way the students responded to the father and David's situation.

> Mr Murray is a stuck-up snob who won't let his son do anything and would also snort at things. He didn't care about anything and had no respect for anyone. (Jason)

> David's father didn't think too much of his son. He was always criticising David when David was young and was just having fun – like all young children do. David's dad wanted David to grow up too fast. I don't really like David's father because he only thinks of himself and he sounds really mean towards the way he treats David. David's dad doesn't care about himself, like the time when David's sister started crying and he abused her which made her more upset . . . I also feel that David's dad is very violent like how he was going on and shouting when he said the possum should be shot . . . Maybe he got this type of aggression and feelings because maybe he was in the army – in war. I feel sorry for David because he was trying to make his father proud of him but was always failing. (Jeremy)

While Jason emphasises Mr Murray's class position in influencing his treatment of David, Jeremy interprets the father's behaviour as an effect of his army experiences which are not explicitly or even implicitly referred to in the text. In fact, many of the boys, despite rejecting the father's treatment of his son as cruel and inappropriate, attempted to find a cause for his behaviour or to explain his violence.

Other students made the point that David was a lonely boy and tended to emphasise the extent to which he was restricted and trapped:

> *I think David was really a quiet and lonely boy, not knowing very much about life and the outside world. He was not even permitted to play with his friends.* (Justin)

> *I think David's father is a selfish pig and he should start letting David do the things that he wants to. I don't like David's father and he should let his son have more freedom.* (Adrian)

> *David's father showed no care for his son, limiting his freedom as a child to go out and play with his friends. The father restricts David's friends because of the humiliation about his accent and he has to play with his sister using dolls as their playing ingredient. His father showed no feeling towards his family and he only cares about himself. His father has been described as a pig by his daughter in the way he killed all those animals with no feelings and slaughtering them which made her cry . . . David's father is aggressive . . . David is scared of his father and his dad wanted him to grow up as a man.* (Sean)

> *'The Altar of the Family' by Michael Wilding deals with issues to do with society putting pressure on younger generations. In this case the young boy David likes to do alternative things rather than what society says he should do, e.g. you're only a real man if you play cricket and you're a pansy if you play with dolls. David's father, in a way, is a stereotyped Aussie male, e.g. wants his son to be a man and to do manly things. He strongly disagrees with what David does in his past time and he calls him all sorts of things to put his son down for being an individual.* (Gary)

However, the class discussion was not all smooth sailing. Some of the boys still tended to find David's behaviour questionable and read his playing with dolls as an indicator of homosexuality.

One boy made the comment that, sure, the father was a 'dickhead', but still he didn't approve of David playing with dolls 'because it seemed gay'. At this point I asked the rest of the class whether they agreed that playing with dolls meant that you were gay? Interestingly enough, it was the girls who responded to this question claiming that it was unfair to judge David in this way since he was just a boy. Some of the boys conceded, but then replied that after a certain age, however, they would consider such behaviour to be abnormal.

One of the boys made the comment that he felt he could talk about his emotions with his girlfriend but that he did not feel comfortable doing so with his mates. This led to a discussion about when it was appropriate for men to express their emotions. One boy also made the point that it was only acceptable for men to cry and to express what they were feeling to one another only if there were a crisis. Under other circumstances they considered such behaviour 'poofy'.

> *If someone has died, etc., it's okay, but men who just express what they are feeling for the sake of clearing their minds are seen as sissies.*

Other issues arose. We discussed the policing of masculinity. I asked the class whether they thought it was okay for two men to show affection for one another in the same way that girls do. They claimed that for the most part any display of affection or intimacy amongst boys would be read as a sign of gayness. On this point the boys and the girls were unanimous. The exceptions they raised related to crisis situations involving the death of someone close. In this situation hugging was seen in the context of offering comfort to a friend.

I remember walking out of that lesson thinking that I had achieved something. Sure, there had been some resistance. Some students had produced homophobic responses and had seemed quite fixed in their views. But, at the end of the day, I really felt that I had been able to use the short story to challenge dominant and accepted ways of thinking about gender and masculinity. At least, I thought, I had got them to consider the effects of oppressive gender stereotypes in a way that they did not find confronting or threatening.

Wayne Martino is an English Teacher at Corpus Christi College, Bateman in Perth, Western Australia. He has taught in secondary schools for ten years, holds an Honours Research Master's Degree in Education and is currently undertaking doctoral studies at Murdoch University where he is conducting research into the links between masculinity and learning in schools. He has recently co-authored (with Bronwyn Mellor) *Gendered Fictions*, a textbook for English teachers published by Chalkface Press, which focuses on the construction of masculinity in texts.

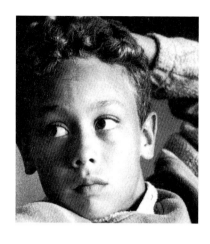

Young and powerful

Maureen Moran, cofounder of a new school in Lismore, describes the fears, struggles and joys of working with boys who (beneath their tough exteriors) desperately want to be valued.

young and Powerful is the result of a vision that Annie McWilliam and I shared four years ago. We had always felt that unless the emotional needs of young people were addressed as a priority in their educational experience then very little was going to change for them, for the adults they were to become and, therefore, for our society in general.

We designed a program which we called 'Young and Powerful', borrowing the name from a young people's Re-evaluation Counselling magazine. For the last four years we have been using it in our work with young people from the ages of five to eighteen.

Quite early in our work we discovered the importance of working frequently with separate gender groups as it allowed us to identify issues which otherwise remained masked. Both of us have been quite profoundly affected by what we have learnt from young men – about ourselves, our beliefs as women working with boys and about them. We have been allowed to see how deeply, consistently and repeatedly they are hurt, how ready they are for someone to reach out to them and the magnitude of the changes that can occur when someone comes in close and stays with them.

Getting close – the key to our work

One of the earliest things we noticed in our relationships with boys was that we didn't touch them anywhere near as much as we touched the girls. These particular young people with whom we were working attended a community primary school. The gender issues we encountered there were small in comparison with our later work in State schools. The boys were often relaxed and friendly around each other, reasonably physically close and had good relationships with most of the girls.

When we considered what was happening for us, we realised that we were much more likely to hug and kiss the girls – as they were constantly physically close and affectionate. When we did hug the boys they would, at best, stand still with their arms hanging and tolerate us. They figured we would give up, as this is what people often do around boys – including us. We could hear all the old stereotypes: 'Boys are rougher', 'They don't like being hugged and kissed and all that stuff', etc.

Luckily we knew that was rubbish. We were seeing the pictures that the boys had of themselves. There are myriad ways these pictures get put in place.

We needed to get close to them in ways that didn't make them shut down. So we got a lot more physical. With one particular boy (who was very mistrustful, a fighter in every school he had been to, and often sullen and angry), one of us would tackle him to the floor and kiss him all over the head. He would shriek and laugh and struggle and wrestle with us. We never, ever overpowered him; we matched ourselves so that he was always physically in charge. Every day as we arrived at school he would greet us with a delighted, beaming face as he pretended to be horrified by the fact that we would probably hug and kiss him. We built up this relationship over a period of three years.

We made a conscious decision to notice the physical contact we made with the boys. We stayed close even when they appeared totally indifferent. This connection might have been simply our hands resting on their backs, an arm around a shoulder or a long hug. We would pick up their arms and wrap them around us and say, 'Grip, grip! Let's feel some grip happening here!'.

Everything would be aimed at connecting them with us, even for a moment. And it worked. The boys began to be softer with each other, to sit with us or on our laps when they needed to cry, to lean against us when we sat next to them, to touch our hands, to come back.

> One boy had a difficult relationship with his father from whom he had been separated (on and off) during the eleven years of his life. We had done quite a lot of talking with the father and the son. However it became apparent that it was hard for the dad to stop analysing and for the son to stop being cold and angry.

> One day we were sitting with them and, on an impulse, Maureen held the boy's face very gently and rubbed his nose against his dad's. He wept and wept as if his heart would break. It was still hard for the father to reach out for him – however, the son was able to show how much he hurt rather than hide behind the 'unreachable' mask he usually wore.

Whatever happened to playing?

Our aim of getting close led us to look at playing and young people. Again we organised separate gender groups as well as mixed.

> I remember standing on the verandah at school waiting for everyone to come in from lunch. Things had been changing over a few months. All the older girls (Years 5 and 6) had stopped going to play soccer and touch footy with the boys. At first I thought it was the beginning of the lethargy that appears to set in with puberty, possibly as a result of internalised sexism. However, when asked, the girls said they refused to play because the boys were so abusive and cranky – particularly if the girls made a mistake.

> I looked at the boys' faces as they came down from the playing field this day. Their expressions were grim, anxious, unhappy and angry. We talked with them and asked them if they were enjoying playing together. They were not. One of our oldest boys had recently left to go to high school. He had been an exceptional young man, noncompetitive, a great sportsperson, incredibly supportive and fun to play with. Our next two oldest boys did not

have an easy relationship with playing and the dynamic amongst the boys was deteriorating.

We couldn't figure out what to do. So, as an interim measure, we put a stop to all sports-type games. Everyone now had to play on the play areas near the classrooms rather than being isolated up at the top of the school. There were some strong and angry feelings. However within two days we had thirty-five young people of all ages (nearly the whole school) playing 'One-two-three home' together, laughing and shrieking with very few upsets. All the young people were playing together again.

We tried several different ways of supporting the boys so that things would go well when they played their more traditional games. Unfortunately not much really worked, except having plenty of adults playing with them who did not get competitive. This was rarely possible. Sometimes we would all play together and I would cheat outrageously, trying to lighten-up their seriousness. The girls would laugh, so would some boys – but others would throw their equipment to the ground and walk off.

What became apparent to us was that the issues around boys and sport were extremely complex. It was an important realisation for us to appreciate the range of feelings produced by the boys when they played: their expectations and disappointments, the pressures, performance-anxiety, tension and numbness to how confused and hurt they were.

We have always believed that boys' participation in sport from an early age creates a rigid 'us and them' attitude; a complete dehumanising of the 'other'; a heavy, heavy performance pressure with little tolerance of mistakes combined with the oppressive load of knowing that if they stuff up they will have blown it for the whole team. On a daily basis they are always out to beat some other male. In the long term they are conditioned to participate in war, if necessary, where they will have to kill another young person, who they must never notice is just like them.

Diametrically opposed to this is the (unfortunate) reality that only within sporting activities are boys able to have some type of closeness with other boys without the risk of being called a 'poof'. To take this away from them and not replace it with something else can feel (to them) like life and death.

My son Jeremy would sometimes come to me at home or school and say, 'Mum, could you tell us we can't play sport again for a while. It is getting really horrible again, and I am being awful too. I don't like it'.

So I would. My son is twelve years old. He has never played competition sports and has always attended noncompetitive schools. He is an exceptional athlete and quite talented at any games he chooses to play. At the moment he loves basketball, roller-blading, cricket and touch footy. However, while he and his friends are playing, I can see their faces change, their voices get angry and their language become attacking. So we give their game-playing close attention: we keep talking to them, help them notice what is happening for them, encourage them to think about why this is so and constantly offer them alternatives.

Wrestling and noncompetitive games

One of these alternatives is wrestling. At the primary school at which we worked we would let all the boys (about twelve in all) leap on us and wrestle with us in a bunch. The first time there were quite a few minutes of stunned disbelief, then they flung themselves on us. There were a few rules: we would limit the time for wrestling if we felt it was necessary, and 'Stop' always meant 'Stop'.

We would also wrestle a few boys at a time. Unfortunately we could never seem to do it enough for them. It was a great way to get close, to scream and laugh and for us to stop acting like adults. They got to play hard physically in a way that didn't involve them hurting or getting angry with each other, or having to worry about winning or losing, as it was usually Annie and I who looked battered and dishevelled by the end of it!

Something else we have learnt is that boys who are very skilful, physically, need to take time to notice their achievements and not just rush on to the next, more difficult feat. We help them appreciate how wonderful it feels to be strong and physically capable. Boys are expected to be fit and strong – yet there is a conflict. They do not want to be seen to be sexist or 'macho', and (at the same time) their fear is that what they have achieved is never enough because someone else is probably doing better –

and if they are proud of themselves then they're 'wankers'! Not a lot of room to move here!

So with us they get to delight in how well they are doing and how well their friends are doing. And they are allowed to acknowledge their feelings – of being scared, disappointed or (most fearful of all) being thought of as a 'wuss'.

What a contrast and relief it is to just play – especially compared with the intense nature of competitive sport which has become the bulk of a lot of young people's play. In our new school we don't call anything 'sport'. We have games: every game you can imagine, from 'Cat and Mouse' to drama games, simulation games, leg wrestles, sock wrestles, pillow fights and charades. We also go rock climbing, abseiling, bowling and skating (and there will be things we haven't thought of yet).

Our aim is to have fun, get close and build relationships. We have to make sure that our young people have a lot of close-playing, together, in between attempts to play the more traditional sporting games. This way it will become harder for them to take the game so seriously that they forget that they know each other and that winning is *not* the aim. It also maintains the very important reality that young people do play together well.

Special Year 10 programs

At one school we developed a special program for Year 10 students where we worked with a group of thirty-five, splitting this into separate gender groups. Because of the dynamics that exist between boys and girls in high schools, we felt that creating group safety in a mixed group was less likely, given the short amount of time we had.

> *Prior to our first all-boys class I was feeling a little daunted – a bit frightened of one or two of the boys – and thought we might need a big male presence working with us, just in case they got way out of line and we had to jump on them! I realised that this was not a useful way to think about these young people. Partly I was reacting to information we had been given by the school. Our group had some pretty tough boys – the playground fighters and the trouble makers. Young people of colour were in both*

groups. Also we had listened to some disturbing, homophobic comments from some of the boys.

I was able to figure out quickly that what I was feeling were my own fears – and nothing to do with these young men. Also I realised that it was very important that I went to this first all-boys class completely relaxed, ready to be delighted in them and willing to get close and make mistakes.

Things went extremely well. It didn't take long for these young men to realise that we were going to listen to them without criticism, put-downs or interruptions. Once that happened, they took us very quickly to the places where life was hard for them. I am constantly startled at how close below the surface lie the vulnerabilities, confusion and lovingness of boys. While the outside may be daunting (to say the least), if you reach past that, they take you in, ask for help and show you where it hurts. The school was amazed that hardly any student ever missed a group and that we even liked *the young people.*

The way we worked

When we work with groups we have the same set of agreements: no put-downs, no cross-talking, no commenting on what other people say and complete confidentiality. These four agreements are rarely broken. Young people are amazed when we tell them that all the adults in the room also must keep the same agreements.

During our time with these boys we looked at self-esteem and conflict resolution and listened to their hopes and dreams. We told them often how much we liked them and how we loved working with them. We gave them strategies for dealing with the school environment – well-meaning (at times) but actually oppressive. We also worked with them on speaking a little differently with each other. We held out the possibility that the sarcasm and put-downs they loved so much as forms of communication were the safest and best ways they had found to say they liked each other. We respected them, and they showed us how completely intelligent, thoughtful, loving and good they were.

We also did some good work on homophobia. When feelings came up about homosexual men we let the discussion continue without censoring their comments. Then we shared our information and feelings, and often we could see them rethinking some of their ideas. They began to see the connection between fear being used to keep men from being close to each other and how the fear of homosexuality has been a key tool in this process.

The boys in our group played with real delight. It was an amazing sight to see twenty sixteen-year-old boys in a State school classroom playing 'Cat and Mouse' and passing oranges to each other under their chins. When some of them were worried they might be seen, we had to pull the blinds down for the second game. This proved a useful discussion point because many of the boys commented on the fact that this was exactly what we had been talking about: people might think they were 'queer' if they saw them playing this way.

We also leg-wrestled with them. The two of us always wrestle together first to show how it is done – and also because it brings most young people to a standstill to see two adults lying on the floor, leg-wrestling.

Affirming their worth

For us, we look back on two things we said in particular that had a deep impact on the whole group. The first was an affirmation we gave them to say to themselves when they were being harassed by a teacher or another adult: 'No matter what you say or do to me, I am a worthwhile person'.

We created a role-play in which we acted like angry teachers. Most of them stood with their heads down, hands in pockets, shuffling. Then we asked them to say the phrase to us. The changes in tone, posture and facial expressions were dramatic. The more they said it the stronger and clearer they became. You could see it sinking in: this was *the truth* about them. (We talked about the fact that it was probably more useful for them to say it in their minds because, otherwise, not all adults might react well.)

The second memorable moment occurred as a result of the boys talking about themselves. They nearly always felt they were no good. What came through strongly was that they really wanted to be good and to get things right.

So we told them that they were completely good, that they always had been completely good and that they always would be completely good. The room went totally silent. We repeated it again. Their faces said it all: it had been such a long time since they had even *felt* that truth to be a possibility.

Witnessing real change

Another high point was a trip to an outdoor ropes program for three days. The boys were able to put a lot of what we had been discussing into practice. In particular, their conflict-resolution skills were required in the case of a difficult teacher (who accompanied us) and one of the trainers on the course.

> *I cried with fear during one of the activities that really terrified me. The boy behind me pushed through his own enormous fear and actually kept encouraging me. His few words may not have seemed like much to someone watching but it was huge for him.*

For one of the other boys it was the first school trip in four years during which he had not got into serious trouble. (This did require us to intervene between him and an adult on a few occasions, but he always worked with us and realised that he could take charge.)

We still see many of the boys around town; and they sometimes drop in to see us at our new school. Although we are occasionally unsure about the effectiveness of working with them over such a limited period, these concerns are dispelled every time we see them. A wonderful connection is still there: their faces light up as they eagerly tell us how they are doing and what has been happening for them.

We take heart from comments the boys made after our groups:

> *'I am more awake and happy – don't know why – waiting for something and really relaxed';*

> *'I'm happy now';*

> *'I feel relaxed from talking to Maureen and Annie';*

> *'The more time I spend in this group the more I'm awake and enthusiastic';*

> *'After this group thing, I'm feeling happy about something – and more alive, like my heart's pumping and I haven't just woke up from the dead'.*

The Young and Powerful School

At the beginning of 1995 we opened the Young and Powerful School for students from Year 4 to Year 9. At the moment it is mostly boys. Again, our work with the older boys in particular has had the most startling results. They have a deep need to know they are good. Some have hidden for so long behind a smart-arse, sarcastic, 'cool-to-be-fool' facade that they are terrified no-one will step in, reach behind and help them out.

Ironically, they probably got into that syndrome through fear of being so badly humiliated, bashed or hurt (emotionally) that, for many, they feel like they might die. So we patiently stay with them. They struggle and yell – and get scared, delighted, confused and unsure. And we stay steady – and show that we do care for them and believe in them and that it is easy to see how good they are.

Some of them have almost hidden from the 'other' boys in their world who look like all the stereotypes about boys and men that they desperately don't want to be like. They get confused about what being a boy is – what to give up and what to keep – and are unsure about whether they are bad when they become noisy and rough.

In their confusion, we try to figure out ways to get close to them, to always be pleased with them – particularly when they are 'difficult'. We work with all of them, looking at how stereotyping hurts them, how sexism hurts everybody and how wonderful it is to be male.

A new little girl started at the school and she was standing next to our oldest boy at the bag hooks, looking quite scared. I said to her, 'Ben is a lovely boy and he won't hurt you. You are quite safe with him'.

He just looked at me and said, 'No-one has ever said that about me before'.

I sat in our school lounge-room two days ago and watched Ryan holding six-year-old Jessie's new baby doll. He held it close to him and stroked its head as he listened to what we were talking about. I looked around our 'Young and Powerful' class and saw Jeremy and Johti holding hands with their fingers entwined. I saw someone fall over in a game, and one of our boys comfort the hurt person, take them inside and look after them. I watched three of them walk around inside an upside-down washing machine box. I saw my thirteen-year-old daughter tackle one of the boys to the floor and listened to them make more noise than I ever thought possible as they revel in this experience of getting close to each other.

I like it that we can give these young men a chance to see themselves again and create enough safety so they can risk deciding to act from their true selves.

Maureen Moran has worked extensively with young people for eleven years as a teacher and counsellor. Her teaching work has mainly been in alternative educational settings. In her counselling, she has established support groups and counselling classes and encouraged leadership amongst young people.

Maureen Moran and Annie McWilliam see educational change as a fundamental component of social change. They view the creation of the 'Young and Powerful' programs and the Young and Powerful School as the ways in which they will realise their visions.

Being 'cool' and a reader

Gwenda Sanderson, a leading specialist in literacy and learning, explores a range of successful approaches which develop a love of reading in boys and help them redefine their views of acceptable male behaviour.

Words of advice from an eleven-year-old boy [who *is* 'cool' and a reader]

If you really want your son to read
Get him the sort of book
Some parents don't seem to see.
It's all about image and being cool
And a lot depends on what you read at school.

Bugulugs Bum Thief
Goosebumps
Point Crime
Paul Jennings
The list goes on.
At least they are not glued
To a Nintendo playing Donkey Kong.

So take my advice
And you'll feel quite proud
Please don't make them read aloud.
If you do
They'll quit reading like a flash
And your reading scheme
Will fall down with a crash.

So if you take my tips
And do everything right
Your son could be reading
By tonight!

Robert Chaseling

Boys who are not reading

Evan, ten-year-old school captain and sports champion, was referred to me because he was falling behind his peers at school. He was an intelligent, friendly, responsible boy. He was well liked by his peers and had excelled in swimming and soccer. He admitted he was more interested in sport than school.

Evan had read scarcely any full novels by himself. Most of the books he had 'read' had been read to him by a teacher or his mother. He was reading hesitantly several years below his age level, and his writing was full of invented spellings. He was afraid to take risks in either his reading or his writing. Evan was classified as 'learning disabled'.

I administer and teach at a private educational centre where children attend weekly lessons after school to receive extra support with their learning. Eighty-five percent of these students are boys. Evan's story is not unique. Nearly every day I have calls from a teacher or a parent who describes the problems a boy is having with his English and, without my prompting, the line will just come into the conversation, 'Of course, I can't get him to read', or 'He really doesn't enjoy reading'.

My observation of the reading habits of the hundreds of Year 6 students I've taught over the past twenty years is that the *average* boy reads half to one novel a week (i.e. a 28 000–45 000 word book, such as *Boy* by Roald Dahl, *Unbearable* by Paul Jennings or *Redwall* by Brian Jacques), whereas the average girl reads one to two novels.

The top quarter of the class, who are mainly girls, are reading two to ten novels a week, and the lowest quarter of Year 6, who are mainly boys, are not reading novels at all. When these boys choose to read by themselves, they are reading bridging books of 400–1000 words such as the *Jets* or *Skinny* series. These books are designed for readers who are reading at the level between picture books and novels. They may read books of 3000–5000 words such as Paul Jennings' *Gismo* or *The Paw Thing*, comics or joke books. Some of this group now read one of the popular *Goosebumps* titles over several weeks.

This increasing difference in the quantity of reading done by boys and girls then significantly impacts on the educational levels of both groups.

Inexperienced readers, not constitutionally deficient

The boys I work with are as smart and capable as any girl. They are, in most cases, *inexperienced* readers. A ten-year-old boy such as Evan had probably read a fraction of the amount that his sister or the girl who sits beside him in class had read at the same age. I believe this experiential gap reflects in the educational levels of boys in comparison with girls.

The pattern is that the parents of a boy like Evan notice their son resisting or having difficulty in reading and writing, particularly if they have older children. They may liaise with the teacher, who also expresses concern about the boy's progress. The parents may then look for an outside 'expert' opinion to find out why their boy is not performing to expectation.

Commonly, boys who are more than several years behind at school, and who are uninterested and reluctant readers, are labelled by school counsellors or psychologists as having a 'learning difficulty' or a 'learning disability', 'dyslexia' or an 'attention deficit disorder'. When practitioners start with the assumptions behind the labelling, they are necessarily constrained by a set of traditional remedial practices. In my experience these programs do not help boys in the long term. In the short term, such approaches quickly bore most boys and further consolidate their view that reading is not for them.

By focusing on the pathology of boys, we situate the problem in a physical–cognitive abnormality, or as a difference between girls and boys. Thus the current explanations of literacy-learning failure and lack of interest have not sufficiently focused on boys' gender expectations and the stigma attached to being seen as a keen reader. I believe that reading provides a source of tension for boys, and that this becomes the most significant factor in their decreased reading, and their consequent underachievement.

Reading changes boys' lives

Reading books is of paramount importance for boys, not simply in terms of school achievement, but because books and reading enhance their lives. Reading literature affects the way we think, what we understand about the world, and the way we 'nurture our soul'. Books can inspire us and expand our horizons. Boys need books for inspiration for images to think with. With books, boys can explore the diversity, complexity and strangeness of human experience.

I have seen boys write in their reading response journals that a book such as Tim Winton's *Lockie Leonard Scumbuster* or Christobel Mattingley's *No Gun for Asmir* or Murray Heasley's *Shuz* has had such an impact on them that they will never be the same after reading that book. They saw life through another person's experience and that vicarious experience changed them. They see other boys in stories coping with adversity, resolving interpersonal conflict or acting against stereotypes that are embedded in popular culture. Most profoundly, from an academic perspective, reading books accelerates a student's academic levels. Boys who read little, risk underachievement in most areas of the school curriculum.

Teachers' views about boys' resistance to reading

I recently asked a group of primary teachers to write what they saw as the reasons why boys read less than girls. All explanations revolved around boys' active nature ('boys do things, girls are content to sit and read'), boys' greater obsession with sport, or a criticism of existing literature as not meeting boys' interests. One teacher stated that there were few books suited to boys. These beliefs are commonly expressed, but in my view they are limited.

Boys 'do' things

The first explanation reflects the reality of the playground environment where boys are to be seen taking up the larger physical area at school, chasing each other or playing sport. In contrast, girls often sit around the edge of the play area, engaging in quieter pursuits, frequently reading a book. To this extent, boys and girls are play-acting out the powerful metaphors of what it means to be male or female in our society. It is almost as if the passive act of reading and physical activity are mutually exclusive domains.

Boys' interest in sport and other things

This is also true. Outside school, boys have a great many other interests that books must compete with, such as sport practices and events, computers, videos, TV, bike riding, skateboarding and just 'mucking around outside'.

Involvement in organised sport can become an obstacle to school success for boys, both by the few who are winners and the large majority who are not winners. Sport is seen by many parents as the pathway to achieving male identity and self worth. Some parents identify their son's sporting prowess and success as the sole source of his self-esteem.

Limited boys' books

In reality, there are more books for boys than for girls. The research in this field continues to show that stories generally contain more boys than girls, that central characters are mainly boys, and that stereotyped versions of 'boys' interests' – e.g. sport, wars, adventure – predominate.

As teachers, we need to expand our understanding around boys' resistance to reading, beyond boys choosing to do other things. By exploring boys' gendered notions about the act of reading, we can support boys to become readers.

Boys' views about themselves as readers

When I asked Mark, aged ten, about boys and reading, he said, 'Boys are always doing what they want. Boys, when they have something to do, they just do it. Girls take more time and they just sit around. Boys are always active. I only read a book when I'm made to. When I'm bored I just sit there and do nothing, like watch TV, whereas Sarah (his sister) always reads. I don't think my friends read much.'

> *Recently I asked eight eleven-year-old boys to give me a profile on a boy their age who is 'cool' and one who they would see as a 'wuss'. (I had been increasingly aware of their use of the opposing terms.)*
>
> *The boys gave me a list of synonyms for 'wuss' which included loser, a dweeb, an idiot, a dork, a drip, a moron, posh, a pussie, a douche, a girl, a girl lover, a wimp, a wanker, queer, gay, happy, gay farts, weird, a donkey brain, and twinkle toes. The boys chose whichever synonym they wanted and gave me a written list of what a boy in either category wears, says, how he behaves, what he reads for pleasure, what girls think of him, how many there were in their class, and which category they wanted to be in.*
>
> *A 'wuss' wears 'posh' clothes like a white shirt, black trousers and black polished shoes. His speech is normal. He doesn't get into trouble at school, and he's a 'goodie-goodie'. He reads all the time, everywhere, and reads books that are thick or 'for adults' and magazines such as CSIRO's* Double Helix. *They thought girls saw 'wusses', as 'geeks', 'stupid', 'losers', 'queer', or as 'a mirror of themselves'. There were between zero and four in their classes at school. And, uniformly, the boys all wanted to be 'cool'.*
>
> *So what does a 'cool' guy look like to these boys? The replies included wearing homeboy pants or board shorts, surf brand name clothes and basketball boots. A 'cool guy' may muck up at times, get into fights and get himself into trouble. The 'cool' guy doesn't read or seldom reads. When he does read, it's horror or murder stories, magazines, comics, cereal boxes or 'good books'. This guy is considered 'the best' by the girls. Most of the boys saw the majority of the boys in their class as 'cool'.*

My concern is that many boys perceive reading as both passive and feminine, and are therefore alienated from what reading is about. It seems to me that their concept of masculinity is easily thrown by 'doing' literacy, and being like a 'female'. To see the cause of boys' resistance as inadequate or different cognitive processing of linguistic information, i.e. pathological, or to blame current reading material as not meeting boys' needs, is to obscure the social reality of their lives and the set of values these boys hold about maintaining their maleness.

Boys' limited involvement in reading and their consequent underachievement will continue unless we actively encourage boys, as well as girls, to move beyond gender stereotypes and the continued denigration and inferiorisation of anything female. Reading and maleness are not incompatible entities.

Girls' views about boys as readers

The boys' explanation of and identification with 'cool' really opened my eyes. I was keen to get the views of a group of ten to eleven-year-old girls that I work with. (I know how boys of this age want to impress the girls.)

Katie suggested that, 'Girls read more. Boys just don't like reading. They'd rather do other things like play chess or have thumb wars. Only the posh ones read. The cool ones don't read.'

I was dumbfounded to hear the same categories 'posh' and 'cool' used by girls. Monique's older brother had been my student for three years and has subsequently been placed in the top Year 8 class at high school. Monique volunteered, 'Yeah, my brother reads all the time. He's posh. He just likes reading.'

So I asked the girls who they'd prefer – a 'cool' boy or a 'poshie'. No votes for 'posh'. Without hesitation all votes were for 'cool'. Madeleine qualified her selection, 'Well I'd want cool and honest and caring,' as if those two qualities weren't necessarily part of the make-up of the regular 'cool' guy. Tanya added, 'Yeah that's what I want, too. You know, boys don't read proper books. They read sports magazines and stuff like that. The girls in our class are always reading novels.' Kara's view was that, 'The boys just aren't interested. They play up in reading. They get out of doing it.'

Boys value girls' opinions, so when I realised that the girls placed a similar value on 'coolness', I began to see why this problem is so difficult to resolve. It is framed by such a persuasive set of values, held by both boys and girls.

Fathers' involvement in their sons' reading

There are conflicting messages about males and reading in the public and private arenas. While encouraged to read at school, boys may have significant males in their lives who do not value reading. Boys often refer to the females in their homes as readers. They say that their fathers and other brothers spend their free time involved in sporting events, watching sport on TV or in other active nonreading pursuits. This conflicting information about what being masculine or literate *looks like*, challenges boys and creates a tension.

Many fathers speak with pride and interest of their boys' sporting involvements and accomplishments. In social settings there is less spoken enthusiasm for their sons' academic achievement and, in particular, their involvement in reading. In some cases, reading is directly opposed to the masculine identity. At a parent–teacher meeting, a kindergarten teacher was encouraging parents to foster their children's reading at home. During the coffee break, she overheard some father's comment: 'As long as he can chuck a ball around the field, he'll be right' and 'I don't want my son to be a sissy'. For these fathers, who undoubtedly wanted their sons to do well at school, reading books was seen as a potential threat to their son's masculine identity, represented by achievement in sport.

I have contact in person or by phone with about five percent of the fathers at my centre. Mothers predominantly initiate the first contact and subsequent phone calls concerning their boys' ongoing progress and any organisation changes. They deliver and pick up their children. Most of these mothers work full-time, so it is not that the mother has more time. It is simply seen as 'the wife's domain' and reflects the gendered division of labour and responsibilities in the home.

Fathers' distancing and estrangement from such an important area of their boys' lives have to be addressed. The echo of fathers' physical and psychological absence is sometimes apparent in the stories shared by boys and their mothers. Often this distancing is because of the ongoing financial constraints of 'outside' work. I've heard fathers lament their lack of involvement with their sons on the basis of working so hard to provide adequately for their family. This is an unenviable position, but it still needs to be addressed by fathers. It is too easy for fathers to forfeit an intimate knowledge of their sons' schooling, and thereby miss out on an opportunity to support their boys.

We need to target increased father-involvement in school literacy projects, such as parent tutoring. When I was teaching in a school setting, I was always so delighted to have dads come to evening school meetings where literacy was the topic of discussion. I'm sure these fathers were very influential in their sons' learning. When I look back over my years of teaching, at the boys whose fathers were physically and emotionally involved in supporting their sons' education, my observation is that these boys took off more dramatically, when given the extra learning support.

We need to encourage mothers to see reading materials other than books as being legitimate reading. Sometimes the scope and quantity of a father's personal reading may be dismissed, when in fact, he may read three major papers over the weekend, his weekly *Bulletin* from cover to cover, and spend hours at the computer composing and reading documents. All of this may be outside the considerable volume of reading he does in his work away from the home.

It is important that mothers don't set fathers up to be seen in front of the children as 'nonreaders'. It is also possible that men do not see personal novel reading as an option for leisure because of the stigma of it being seen as a 'passive' and therefore female activity.

I've seen boys really act on their father's suggestion about a good book. I once had a dad who used to love reading his son's books. He'd often read them the very night they came home, and his son, Jason, would say next week when I saw him, 'Dad *loved* that book, so I read that one first, and 'Dad said that one wasn't as good as X author's first book, so I left that one till last night to read'. It meant such a lot to him, to think he was choosing books for him *and* his dad to read.

Challenging boys' resistance

(I should add to this heading: 'and supporting them to become readers who are also "cool"'.)

So how can we acknowledge a boy's desire to be 'cool' and, at the same time, involve him in a pursuit that may conflict with his resistance to reading and his personal interests, as well as his very notion of what constitutes maleness?

When I work with boys like Evan, I utilise some of the following principles and practical strategies.

Be a reader yourself

I read widely for my own pleasure. I read the books I want them to read. I constantly look for and read the books that might get them reading. I scour magazines such as *Magpies, Rippa Reading* and *Reading Time* looking for new titles which may appeal. I frequently ask boys what they are reading and what other boys are reading, hoping to hear of new authors or titles that they are enjoying. It is important to hear what they like to read and not to place my adult values about 'quality' books on them. At first I was not comfortable with stories that seemed weird or even on the gory side, but I soon realised that I couldn't reach boys unless I had an open mind.

I let my boys see me reading during silent reading times during our small group lessons. I show them the book I'm reading at the time and talk about why I chose it. It may be R. L. Stine's latest *Goosebumps* title or *Fear Street* title. They see my excitement, my pleasure at 'settling in for a good read'. My modelling is vital. I believe we can't expect boys to do something that we aren't doing ourselves.

Talk about your own process as a reader

I share what I do when I choose books to read, lose the plot, or come across words I don't know. We call this 'literate talk'. I focus on reading *habits* and not on reading *skills*. Many boys who have got behind at school have had extra skills-based remedial teaching in the reading area which has placed the emphasis on errorless word recall, and not made the enjoyment of the story the focus. I believe such an approach, which is heavily practised in some educational contexts, destroys any possible long term interest in books and reading.

Share 'the cream' of the books

Here I am considering only those books that appeal to boys. I look for books that are funny, that show emotion, that are connected to their own life experiences and that are accessible, i.e. written in an authentic, natural, easy style of writing, where the author's presence is felt, and where the stories are full of action and surprises. Reluctant boy readers are very choosy about what they like to read.

Parents sometimes regale me with lists of books that they have at home, 'and he still won't read'. And they tell me titles of books at home that their daughters loved, or that they have from their childhood, or even books that were award winners. However these guidelines for choosing books for their sons may not be appropriate.

In Australia, some of the most well known book awards are chosen by adult childrens-book specialists, and the choice is based on factors other than whether the book is a 'good read' or not. These judges have to take into account not only the 'literary excellence' of the book, but the way the publisher has produced the book, the appeal of the illustrations as well as the quality of the editorial work on the book itself.

With the KOALA, KROC, and COOL Awards, where children vote for their favourite book each year, the all-time favourite author is Paul Jennings. Yet our most popular children's writer has never won even one major award in the annual prestigious Children's Book Council of Australia Book of the Year Awards, given to books of 'outstanding quality'.

Paul Jennings is often not taken seriously by the children's literature establishment. His humorous, 'lightweight' short-story form has such enduring appeal to boys because it is manageable. This factor is is seemingly not valued when 'literary excellence' is to be judged.

Boys absolutely love the risqué things that happen in Paul's stories. I've seen boys literally howl with laughter on a first reading of one of his stories. When they suddenly come across a boy character who accidentally 'browneyes' a principal, or a boy who has to retrieve his own expensive false tooth from a smelly sewage treatment plant, or a boy, without a stitch of clothing who has to flee from a group of girls, they are hooked!

Books with short paragraphs and short chapters appeal. Most Paul Jennings, Morris Gleitzman and R. L. Stine paragraphs are one to three sentences in length. This is the trend in popular children's fiction, which is to the advantage of boys who are put off by long solid paragraphs covering the page.

When I ask boys how they would help a younger boy having problems with his reading, their main approach is to ensure that the book that they share with such a boy is wildly funny or of the horror/scary vein, such as one of R. L. Stine's.

> *Robert, aged eleven, said, 'You retain your image of being 'in' by reading books like* Goosebumps. *Even if you find them scary in some parts, you don't admit it. You might even pretend in front of other guys that they are not scary at all!'.*

In Robert's case – he's currently reading *The Hobbit,* having just read the 336-page *The Bellmaker,* Brian Jacques' latest *Redwall* story – he's also now moving to authors he's never tried before, such as Elizabeth Hutchins and James Howie. As with most boys, Robert's springboard into books was humorous or scary books. They opened the way for him to get into a wide range of reading. This happens when boys get started into books they can relate to and that they enjoy.

Boys are influenced by the covers of books and when they are selecting new books to read, they seldom look inside the book. For this reason Paul Jennings' amazingly weird covers have appeal, as do the *Goosebumps* titles that look scary. According to the boys I speak with, it's simply 'uncool' to read a book about girls, or a book that has a girl on the cover or even a pink-covered book.

'Walk' with the boys into books

I read aloud to my students – sometimes a few pages, sometimes the first chapter, sometimes the whole book. I want them to 'hear' good writing. I read aloud enthusiastically, sometimes dramatically. I show my own involvement in the story. I laugh; I cry. The only complete books I read aloud to my students are ones by authors whom they have not read before. I also ensure that each boy in a group has his own copy of the book as I read. I am the 'human tie' between them and the author.

I have connected boys with authors in real life or by mail. Having time to actually meet Paul Jennings, Morris Gleitzman, Michael Stephens, and Richard Tulloch in the context of our own space, was a turning point for the boys I was working with at the time. The boys who spent the day as ushers at a Morris Gleitzman author event in my city, and who sat down to lunch with him, later read every book he'd written. I've had boys write to authors such as Roald Dahl (when he was alive) and Murray Heasley, and both authors replied. The letters that came back were extremely important to them. They were treasures that they planned to keep all their lives!

I also act as a mediator for learning about literature and becoming literate. If you like, I am their stockbroker. Boys are handicapped when there is no adult in their life who acts as a mediator around books. They need somebody who knows the stock well.

I hope that our friendship, and the warm and mutually respectful relationship we have, allows each boy to relax enough to unselfconsciously get involved in books that hook him. My role is to be that important connection between the boy and the book. Once he is *in* the book, an author has a chance to win him over.

Discourage reading aloud

No student reads to me or to others unless he explicitly wants to. I encourage them to read at home to themselves, and *only* to their family, if they choose to. Most boys hate reading to a parent, as Robert's poem attests. They feel quite set up and it can so easily become a time of considerable tension between parent and son. I see no educational benefit in making reluctant readers read to their parents. Marcus, aged eleven, informed me that 'a lot of boys get turned off by being made to read to their parents'.

Boys need time to read their own books. They may need support in setting up a home timetable to allow time for their personal reading. This time will give them an opportunity to relax, to be entertained by the book, and to form intimate relationships with the characters in their books. They learn to read by reading. And, the more they read, the more they want to read for their own pleasure.

Encourage parents and other care-givers

Parents need to read to their sons and to read some of their sons' books themselves.

I encourage both parents to see themselves as important role models as readers, to become more book aware, and to talk with their sons about their own personal reading. As I mentioned earlier, I've seen many breakthroughs with previously reluctant readers when a parent has read one of their son's books.

I send home lists of favourite and recommended books. I also suggest using the local library and/or giving books or book vouchers as gifts. It's really important that boys know that their parents see books as being valuable enough to spend money on. A lot of the boys I work with have hundreds of dollars worth of video games, and get to see most major feature films, so they see money being spent on their entertainment and sporting pursuits. They also need to see that their parents place value on book ownership as well.

Encourage them to enthuse each other

Reading is both private and social. Students 'own' their reading when they have the opportunity to share it with others. I'm aware that the first thing I want to do when I finish a good book is to share it with someone else, and encourage them to read it. I provide settings for students to share their reading with their peers. They are 'experts' on the books they've read.

I realise the power of peer influence. I work with the boys in 'boys only' groups. When a boy comes into his lesson on fire about a book he has loved, the others almost 'fight' over it. They are probably more persuaded by each other's recommendations than mine!

> A father told me recently, 'I started reading when I met a friend who was a 'man's man' (at this point he flexed his biceps to show that he meant a real, macho man) who would read three to four books in a day. He'd sit out the back of our flat with the cool tinnies beside him and no-one would bother him. That's when I realised it was 'cool'. It was cool to read!'

Help them challenge the limited male stereotypes in stories

I try to enlighten my students – boys and girls – about the value systems in books. Books are not 'innocent' or 'neutral' windows on real life. I support them in challenging or arguing for the versions of themselves and their worlds that are constructed in the stories. Because the socially constructed roles for males and females in books are often severely limited, I try to encourage their awareness of books where there are alternative and more expansive versions of masculinity, i.e. males who act beyond traditional stereotypes.

> In Shuz for example, the boys in the urban art posse who are the heroes of the story, learn that they don't have to retaliate by beating up the Year 9 gang of thugs to prove their masculinity. A truer test of their personal strength is demonstrated in other, non-violent ways, such as when they initiate a competition to see which gang can run faster, throw straighter or spell better. The females in this

story are not 'bothered' by the male world. They stand up to males physically and verbally. This book absolutely 'hooked' the boys and provided the stimulus for challenging and lively debate about the stereotypes that were maintained or changed by the author. The female characters in this book also expanded the boys' notions of femininity. One of the boys wrote in his journal, 'The author shows that you aren't a girl if you're good at art or if you decide not to fight to fix up your problems'. In this way, fiction can provide a setting to demonstrate that things termed 'feminine' are not necessarily in opposition to their masculinity.

In conclusion

Evan is now fourteen and in an 'A' stream at school. He reads all the time and he's still popular amongst his peers. He is a living example that boys' resistance to reading can be turned around.

What made the difference? I believe that it was by ignoring the labelling and just getting on with the task of encouraging Evan to love books and reading, and helping him to see that reading, as a free-time pursuit, was 'cool' and not a contradiction to his concept of what males do. Evan has expanded his notions of masculinity to include the act of reading for his own enjoyment.

As Robert says in his poem, 'It's all about image and being cool'. When the context and the attitudes are right, boys will give reading and what books have to offer a chance. Then the books themselves and good authors will take over!

And to paraphrase Robert:

So if you take our tips
And do everything right
Your boys could be reading
By tonight!

Gwenda Sanderson is the Director of Arrendell Primary Education Centre in Newcastle (a facility established to provide extra learning support for students) and also lectures in Children's Literature and Literacy at the University of Newcastle. During her twenty-year career Gwenda has worked mainly with boys and is committed to finding ways to help them become lifelong readers. Gwenda has shared her work with teachers and parents locally, nationally and internationally in workshops, conferences, presentations and various writings.

I'll get you at lunch!

How do you deal with boys who use intimidation or physical force to get their way? *Peter Clarke,* an educational psychologist who counsels students with behaviour difficulties, describes the success of his group-work program.

Tony, a Year 5 student, became angry at the slightest problem when relating to other boys in the playground.

'Hey you, get out of my way of I'll thump your head in, stupid!' Tony yelled, as a boy ran across the handball arena.

'Make me, freckle face,' replied Bill, one of the year's heavyweights.

A knife was drawn by Tony and further threats made before the teacher on duty intervened and called for the principal.

This had been their third upset in the week, and neither boy seemed to have the skills to control himself when faced with conflict. However, they were not the only ones in their year with behaviour difficulties.

Tony was suspended for three days. As a consultant teacher for Boys' Education, I was called in to help develop an approach to the incident involving the knife. After his return, I sat in Tony's class to observe the boys' interactions.

'I want the pencils,' demanded Tony of his friend.

'Use your own, boofhead,' was a typical reply. The boys habitually called out in class and demanded their teacher's attention.

'Miss, Tony's being mean and took my pencil case,' complained Bill.

'He wouldn't lend 'em to me, Miss,' Tony spat back.

It was obvious that the boys in this class needed to establish better relationships with each other. They were constantly getting at each other, regularly fighting and hurting themselves and others in the process. The principal, the two class teachers and I decided to organise some intensive group time on a regular basis to focus on relationships and counteract stereotypes about males and conflict. In order to write a program for the group work, I carried out several playground observations. In the meantime, Tony and others were followed up by the school counsellor.

Playground observations

It was fascinating to carry out various playground observations at different times before writing a specific boys program. Using a clipboard and pencil, I started noting in which areas various boys and girls were playing and what types of activities they were engaged in.

In particular, I observed a group of boys who dominated the new play equipment by playing 'touch chasings' (which sometimes resorted to tackle). Whenever the game became too dangerous the teacher on duty would attempt to settle things down.

'Now boys, either you use the equipment properly or you play your game elsewhere,' the teacher calmly said.

'We didn't mean to get carried away, Sir. It won't happen again . . . ,' came the usual reply

Meanwhile a group of girls was huddling in the middle of the equipment reciting a poem and dancing. The boys rebuked them several times but the girls stood their ground explaining that they had as much right as the boys to be there. The boys argued amongst themselves as to what they were going to do. Eventually one of the boys took a leading role and charged at the girls' group. A second boy tried to tackle him.

'You can't do that to the girls!' exclaimed the tackler.

'Why not? They're only girls!' complained the first boy.

'They're not tough enough to handle it,' answered the tackler.

While the boys were arguing, one of the girls jabbed the tackler in the nose, saying, 'Who says we're not?'

The boy, now with a bleeding nose, ran off to the teacher. Meanwhile, the other boys were calling out, 'Sook'. The teacher was quite concerned at the sight of blood and insisted that the boy go to the office to get cleaned up. She remained composed and assured the boy that he need not cry as it was only a 'blood nose'.

'It couldn't have hurt that much,' said the teacher, 'It was a girl who hit you, wasn't it?'

The offending girl was not spoken to and the boys continued their chasings. The boy with the 'blood nose', downhearted and ridiculed, meandered to the office while the teacher continued her roaming.

The implications for staff in this interaction are considerable. These events and others like them occur many times a week. The role modelling provided by staff, particularly male staff, has been found to be important especially for boys lacking social skills. Many of these boys have grown up with inappropriate role models. In order for a program to be successful, it is essential that staff are briefed about the ways they could deal with children.

Working with teachers

The fact that many teachers have responded well to workshops on gender stereotyping suggests that they are aware of the significance of how they interact with students. The main aim of the workshops is for teachers to discover their own biases and to understand the implications of their modelling of behaviour to the children.

Issues that need to be addressed with staff are:
* classroom/playground management and supervision;
* activity-based ideas relating to social skills training; and
* the impact of group work in developing cooperation between boys and between boys and girls.

One of the key phases in any boys program involves staff development and enlisting staff support. A two-hour workshop can have a huge impact on the program's success. Teachers' comments in evaluations reflect this:

'I never thought that I was a hero to some boys.'

'I never thought that group work could achieve so much. If you can help me, I'd like to use it more in my classroom.'

'Negotiating a group contract with primary students . . . you've got to be kidding! When I saw how easy and responsive the kids were – well, I was fascinated.'

Setting up the group-work program

Many of the boys who participated in the group-work program were like Tony. They were not able to keep still for more than five minutes, they often waited for their mates to respond before they did and they pretended in various games that they were Mal Meninga.

We decided it was beneficial for them to spend some time in cooperative small-group activities. In consultation with the class teachers, we divided the boys into mixed peer-groups of eight to ten boys.

One program involved coordinating four separate groups concurrently each week over a ten-week term. Group sessions ran for up to forty-five minutes, whilst the other students were taught by their regular teacher. All the groups were held at various times throughout a day in the same room, which had a large, carpeted area for sitting in a circle on the floor.

One Year 3 teacher wrote a group program with me for his boys. What really impressed me was his drive to maintain an objective: to develop a greater acceptance of individual differences within the class. This was initiated by his frustration in having to spend much time breaking up fights and quarrels between the boys.

Parents would ask him to take their side against another boy's parents. To overcome this, a parent meeting was organised before the start of the program. Parents and guardians were asked to reveal specific behaviours that their sons had displayed in the previous six months. This helped the staff to gain an understanding of the children's behaviour at home. It was also used as a means of evaluation.

Parent response was overwhelmingly positive, and the teacher was less burdened by parent complaints. Once parents were informed of the program, the work with the students could begin. What follows are some key issues in the group-work process that need addressing.

Clarifying the purpose

During the first session, the boys were given a pre-group questionnaire to assess their abilities in writing about their feelings and values. The same questionnaire was administered at the end of the program as a comparison.

After completing this questionnaire, the students were informed of the purpose of the program. An important part of clarifying the purpose was in establishing group rules which were negotiated by the entire group.

In this way, the purpose of such programs becomes clear: to develop a greater acceptance of difference by encouraging boys to work together.

Establishing group behaviour

One of the initial activities for all groups was to establish the group rules and consequences. Tony demanded that the rules be strict, as did most of the boys. (Agreements such as these are best made by voting after a thorough brainstorming session. Consequences are then discussed and decided upon.) In this case, group rules which proved valuable were:

- one person talking at one time;
- try to be honest;
- avoid hitting others and put-downs;
- what happens in the group stays within the group;
- use equipment in the room after gaining permission.

It is difficult for boys to take on new responsibilities in group behaviour. Encouraging this entails careful management of events as they occur. For example:

> 'We'll kiss and make up, Sir, if you like!' says Tony anxiously, whilst the others laughed and called out, 'poof'.

> 'Remember, avoid put-downs. So what do you think, Paul?' I inquire, attempting to encourage honesty.

> *'Bill annoyed Tony. Tony punched Bill. Bill told you,' says Paul thoughtfully.*

The use of questioning and the style of language is important whilst negotiating the group contract. It is a deliberate strategy to demonstrate a model of leadership without using power in order to control the group. This group-work program is a cooperative learning strategy which must be handled skilfully. As a result, staff training is essential.

Building relationships

One of the activities that helped to develop this principle was 'Heroes'. This was a turning point for Tony in his group.

I had asked the boys to bring a picture, model or sketch of their favourite hero to the group. There was excitement in the air as we lined up.

> *'Van Damme is the best.'*
>
> *'No, Arnie's the best.'*
>
> *'Okay guys, let's go in and again sit in a circle on the floor, please.'*
>
> *Tony presented his hero, Michael Jordan, from his basketball card collection.*
>
> *'What is it about Michael Jordan that you like, Tony?' I asked.*
>
> *'I don't know. He's the best.'*
>
> *'Okay, who would like to go next? Robert.'*
>
> *Robert had a photo of his dad working in the garden in his backyard. He explained that his dad was special because he could talk to him about anything.*
>
> *'You sissy,' called out Tony.*
>
> *I warn Tony for calling out at Robert.*
>
> *'What's the problem with Robert having his dad as a hero?' I asked.*
>
> *'I can't talk to my dad about nothing,' says Tony.*
>
> *'Thanks for letting us know you better, Tony,' I reply. Tony drops his head and smiles.*

A second notable session was based on inspiring the students by using a kit of black-and-white photos. We had done some work on expressing feelings in a previous session.

'Peter,' Tony tugged on my shirt, 'I want that photo that Robert has.'

'Have you asked Robert if you can have it or share it?'

'No,' replies Tony anxiously. 'Hey, Robert, can I have the photo of the hang-glider?'

'No, I chose it first,' responds Robert stubbornly.

'I want it, Robert. If you don't give it to me, I'll get you at lunch,' demands Tony.

'Here have it then. There's so many others to choose from.'

'Are you happy with your photo, Tony?' I ask.

'No, I'll take the surfer,' says Tony. He returns the hang-glider photo to the bench.

He explained to me that the only reason he wanted the photo was because Robert liked it so much. I suggested that he say this to Robert – and, astoundingly, he did. He returned the photo and apologised. I could hardly believe what I had heard.

From this session I concluded that the boys had come to feel sufficiently safe to express their true feelings without putting up a screen in front of their peers.

Maintaining interest

I found that to keep the boys interested for each session it was crucial that I varied the pace and the type of activity. It was helpful to have games and access to a wide range of material. Using the stimulation of movement and different work partners in activities helped boys to accept others into their groups.

In order to provide for different learning styles, I used a wide range of visual stimuli and means of expression. Sometimes I would write on the board and at other times use textas on butcher's paper. I would hand out crayons for a drawing activity one time and pencils for a writing activity another time. Also, various sports equipment came in handy; for example, passing around a volleyball in a circle as each boy spoke in turn. This was extremely helpful in developing some cooperation between the boys. It also provided a structure for maintaining the group rules.

So what works?

I believe that group-work (particularly for boys in Years 5 and 6) is a necessary component for their social and educational wellbeing. Such work encourages boys to accept differences in others without resorting to violence and bullying. It is important that:

- boys work together in groups on stereotyping issues;
- staff are suitable role models for these boys;
- classroom and playground observations are made to see what is happening;
- parents are informed of the program and its outcomes;
- staff development takes place;
- there is liaison with a counsellor for critical follow-up of specific cases; and
- the effectiveness of the program is evaluated.

This type of intervention works because it changes the boys' attitudes towards themselves and their peers. They are more prepared to share their feelings and thoughts about how they have behaved. The group-work may not have been successful without some staff development and a negotiated contract at the start. By the end of the course, the boys were able to better control their outbursts of aggression and better able to discuss their problems with their class teachers and friends.

One pleasing outcome of this program was that Tony was able to re-enter the class and begin to work independently. In the playground, he sought other ways of dealing with conflict. One important example was that he recognised that if he walked away, a potential conflict would be diffused. After four months, the staff were most pleased with this change in Tony. No doubt there will be many more boys like Tony in primary schools who could benefit from a group-work program.

Peter Clarke's broad background in teaching has involved him in working in Sydney, Hobart and Darwin, especially with groups of low-achieving and acting-out boys. He has set up several outdoor education programs in schools and works extensively in the area of Boys' Education in Sydney. Peter holds a Masters degree from Macquarie University specialising in behaviour management and is currently an Educational Psychologist with the New South Wales Department of School Education.

Power and classroom relations

The key to changing classroom behaviour lies with students taking more responsibility for their own behaviour and learning. As *Rollo Browne* – an independent consultant in boys' education – explains, this may involve teachers in challenging the very essence of how their classrooms work at present.

 n my work with boys on masculinity and male sexuality I have found that the success of activities and programs relies more on how we are as teachers in the classroom and how we set up and manage classroom relations than on the content. In other words, how it is done as much as what is done. This chapter focuses on four areas related to making such programs work and extending their effectiveness in schools. These are:

- the use of power and the way schools respond to boys' behaviour;
- revealing the need for change to boys;
- working directly with classroom relationships as a key to improving social outcomes in schools; and
- getting men involved in teaching aspects of masculinity and sexuality to boys.

Power issues

The typical way of dealing with unacceptable behaviour by boys in schools is still to punish them. This has the advantage of making the individual responsible for his own behaviour but ignores the critical role of the group in which such behaviour occurs. Punishing boys blames (pathologises) the individual as being a trouble maker and takes no account of the surrounding peer group culture. Often the peer culture supports and rewards disruptive and aggressive behaviour. While teachers and the school frown on certain peer groups, in the past little or nothing seems to have been done about the way those groups operate. It is put into the too-hard basket.

On the other hand, it is becoming clearer that school culture and structure itself maintains aspects of this problematic behaviour. The way the school operates, the way the principal, deputies and teachers model power and authority and reward behaviour, give important messages about what is really important in life and how adults get their needs met. No matter how much we adults talk about respect and fairness, young people are acutely aware of what we *actually do* when we are faced with conflict or difficulty. Schools inevitably model ways of using power and boys seem to be vitally interested in this issue.

The difficulty is that boys frequently behave as if the only valid form of power is *power over* others, or domination. This can be contrasted with *power with* others, or cooperative and representative forms of power. A third form is *power within*, which describes a personally-centred sense of individual power found for example in some martial arts disciplines. When boys only value *power over*, it is inevitable that male aggression, harassment and other unacceptable behaviour will occur.

> At a teacher in-service program on gender and masculinity, a male PE teacher argued strongly against modelling alternative ways of being powerful (seeking power with). 'The boys would laugh at you,' he said. Despite the fact that he saw the link to bullying and aggression, I was unable to convince him to explore alternatives. As he saw it, his school operated quite successfully on a power over system and 'if it ain't broke, don't fix it'. The apparent success of power over systems is at the heart of the difficulty of working on boys' behaviour and masculinity issues within schools, As teachers, we can be creating, modelling and reinforcing the very behaviours that are part of the problem.
>
> A high school deputy described her frustration as follows: 'How can I deal with a boy sent to me for rowdy behaviour when I can't even get the teacher to stop shouting in class?' Schools often create a culture in which bullying, harassment, abuse,

hostility and aggression are but a logical extension of what is being modelled and promoted. Schools do this by spending ten minutes at assembly praising a victorious team and ignoring teams that lose; by a sports coach building aggression before a match and targeting opposition players that need to be 'hit hard', by using grading systems that give students the message that failing is worse than not trying at all. This sets up a system where winning is everything and 'getting the opposition' is rewarded. From here one can see it is not a large step to 'getting someone' in the playground or putting them down in class.

Only recently has much consideration been given to how school structures might support less hostility in classrooms and in the playground.

How can we get boys to see that they have a choice not to accept that *power over* is the be-all-and-end-all of being male? In what less destructive ways could boys meet their need to feel powerful and worthwhile in their own lives? How can they do this without constant power struggles against parents and teachers?

The challenge

The challenge is to work with boys and masculinity so that they see that they do have a choice. We must do more than just change unacceptable individual behaviour. Working to redefine masculinity in a healthier form requires that boys are willing to examine how they construct masculinity on a day-to-day basis, how it is maintained and passed on.

Because such unacceptable behaviours are learned in groups or, at the very least, are maintained and refined in groups, it is important that they are unlearned in groups. Teachers need to take account of the group in teaching about masculinity and power and show how sexism, stereotyping and ideas on male sexuality do affect the way males relate to and think about sex, themselves, each other, women and relationships.

For us as adults the arguments about sexism, sexual harassment and masculinity do make sense. A system or a culture that is discriminatory and depowering is unacceptable. However, the adolescent male viewpoint is different. This is 'just how it is' in the playground and streets. Status is still given to the toughest, quick-witted rebel – one with guts and power.

Why should boys change?

Before we can teach anyone about better ways of getting needs met we first have to get their attention. In workshops I often ask teachers and parents, 'Why should boys listen? After all, they're already doing the best they can, as they see it.'

Teachers and parents come up with a whole range of reasons:
- to get along better with others;
- so they get into less trouble;
- because they are failing in school;
- so they have happier lives;
- so they will be better persons in the future.

Few of these arguments will cut any ice with the boys. The behaviours boys have developed are the finest ways they have of getting their needs met. The fact that some behaviours are quite unsuccessful or that adults find such behaviours objectionable is not the point. When teachers start talking to boys about what goes on behind the carefully constructed image of masculinity, it gets personal. The risks to the boys are higher and there better be good reason to change, otherwise they will just reinforce their stance and defend themselves against yet another critic.

When it comes to ways of rejecting teachers' comments, students are infinitely creative. The credibility of the teacher posing these questions will be called into question. This is where female teachers get labelled as the 'concerned mother', or the 'aggrieved feminist' Likewise, the male teacher may be co-opted as 'one of the boys', or labelled as a 'bossy disciplinarian' telling the boys how to live their lives.

The boys are the ones in control of their behaviour. However, until boys can see the need for change there is likely to be no movement. Like the rest of us, boys may have an interest in maintaining the way things are now. They may get attention, status or just feel they have a place in the world. In working with these issues, the first step has to be one of revealing the need for change. If a power struggle emerges, the opportunity for teaching is lost, particularly when the boys are asked to think about themselves. In introducing a topic on masculinity and male behaviour, the key question to consider from the boys' point of view is: 'What's in it for me?'

Boys seem to respond well when as teachers we work within the following kinds of reasons for change:

- to get needs better met;
- to be successful in relationships;
- to be successful as a sexual being;
- because it's clear that traditional, stereotyped, male attitudes and behaviours that worked previously for men (e.g. fathers) will not work well any more;
- so that boys are not disadvantaged/oppressed;
- so we stop hurting the ones we love.

These reasons are framed in the immediate present so that they apply to boys now. Even so, it is not a foregone conclusion that boys will respond positively. There are no guarantees here.

In the same vein, teachers need to identify what's in it for them to be involved in working to improve boys' behaviour and in boys programs. When asked, teachers talked in terms of less stress and less discipline problems, better classroom behaviour, where students actually listen to each other, so they, the teachers, can spend more time teaching and less time on power struggles with boys. In a nutshell, teachers wanted to feel more successful at their work and saw that an improved quality of relationships in the classroom would mean less harassment, less homophobia, fewer put-downs, less sexism and therefore an improved learning environment for all students.

If boys programs clearly link to teachers' needs then the chance of making progress is significantly higher. Changing a culture is not easy and the benefits must be strongly relevant and immediate for teachers to sustain the effort.

Classroom relationships

At the beginning of any lesson there is a moment in which a teacher needs to grab the initiative and set the tone for the activity. This moment occurs any time an activity is changed or modified. This is also true of any disruptions. Before any power struggle can develop there is a moment where the teacher decides how to assert or reassert control. The adult models a way of getting needs met and sends out messages about what is and isn't important. Often this means bullying and dominating the disruptive element in the class (boys again?) so that order is restored. Students must experience dozens of such moments during the school week. For their part, teachers resent that so much of their time is taken up with classroom management.

> It is in these critical moments that relationships are built and shaped, that power is exercised and modelled, that gender relations are reinforced or challenged. For example, as a first-year-out primary teacher on an Aboriginal settlement and as a tall man, I exerted my presence (voice, size and authority) to get the control I needed. Ten years later, as a sexuality educator running groups in NSW high schools, it was clear that dictating what was to happen was counterproductive. By then I had developed a more participative approach that relied on a different sense of leadership.

Classroom interactions are not just a side issue. They relate directly to learning about the use of power and to learning outcomes of all types. However schools rarely target classroom relationships, preferring to focus on the more measurable areas of curriculum content and discipline.

> We do have an example of where the effects of classroom interaction on student learning were specifically targeted. In this project, teachers were set up in pairs and observed each other in class for twenty minutes a week. They then spent time together inquiring about what each saw at critical moments and examining the teacher's thinking at the time of the interventions. They asked questions such as: 'What does this behaviour tell me about how this person learns?' and 'What have students learned about relating to each other and to adults in this interaction?'

In this process, teachers began looking at student behaviour as an integral part of the learning process rather than a diversion from it.

As the teachers began exploring more deeply into what was happening in their classrooms, they started experimenting with different interventions. They found themselves using broader concepts for understanding classroom dynamics, for example, looking beyond whether behaviour was 'on task' or 'off task'. They made changes in how they taught and intervened. In particular, the teachers began to engage students on the question of how they learn best and in discussions of the students' needs as learners. As a consequence, student behaviour in the classroom changed.

> At the beginning of the project the participating teachers had identified what they most wanted to change in their classrooms:
>
> * to develop a greater autonomy in students so they were less dependent on teachers to initiate and guide learning;
>
> * to engage a wider range of students – e.g. the quiet ones, the disruptive, the bright, the underachieving and those from diverse cultural backgrounds; and
>
> * to make all students more interested in the subject matter and less preoccupied with simply doing what the teacher says (or resisting what the teacher says).

Although they were not talking specifically about boys, the list of changes captures the teachers' desire to shift disengaged or bored students preoccupied with power and status towards taking more responsibility for their own behaviour and for their own learning.

By the end of the project these goals had been achieved.

What made it work?

Firstly the use of observation and feedback sessions by teachers. Once teacher isolation was broken down, the capacity to try out different things in the classroom increased. This was an important tool in shifting teacher focus from the need to control towards working directly with how students learn best. In terms of working with boys' behaviour and attitudes this is a way for teachers to model alternatives to *power over* students.

Secondly, teachers began to read students' outward behaviour for signs of how they might be thinking or feeling as they worked. In particular, they asked students directly what was happening inside at particular points in their learning. This information is highly relevant when a student is having difficulty with a task and expresses this by disrupting others. In these situations, students do not often say what they are thinking and feeling, yet it is precisely what the teacher has to tap into to help the student through the difficulty. Typically, disruptions are a result of boys having difficulty with learning, including boredom, lack of effort, deliberately provoking others. Again the teacher is modelling different responses and avoiding just controlling the disturbance or ignoring the thoughts and feelings of students. This is a critical step in counteracting the ridicule and rejection that dominate boys' relations in many classrooms.

As the project progressed, the teachers described themselves as becoming more patient and less critical of students. They allowed students to express more feelings without feeling personally attacked themselves. The teachers began to deliberately structure classroom activity so that students exercised more choice, worked together more effectively and developed a broader network of relationships. For example, the teacher could set up a project where it was an advantage to pair up with someone who was less academic but street smart. It is true that teachers have to be creative in coming up with questions and topics that will link students across groups around learning. The benefits of classroom relationships are found in students – particularly boys – beginning to learn from and accept each other. This is essential if we are to progress from hostility, bullying, or sexist and homophobic put-downs towards improved gender relations in the classroom. It is no coincidence that the social outcomes achieved in this project directly related to improved academic outcomes.

Social outcomes

One way to get schools to address good classroom and playground relationships coherently is to specify what the school hopes to achieve socially for each student.

> *These are the social outcomes of schooling. For example, by the time they leave school students should be able to:*
>
> - *recognise when they are in conflict with others;*
> - *state clearly (when in conflict) the other person's point of view and feelings;*
> - *find the common ground between different groups and opinions; and*
> - *identify what they might have to learn from someone different from themselves.*

Social outcomes need to be the responsibility of every teacher. Leaving this task to any one group or subject area, such as Personal Development, Health & Physical Education misses the point. It is a school-wide responsibility and is an important step for schools wanting to address boys' behaviour. Few secondary schools have identified key social outcomes which all students are expected to achieve. By contrast, academic and sporting results are frequently mentioned in the various school brochures and capture the values and spirit of the school advertised.

Improving tolerance of difference, reducing harassing behaviour and lifting the level of cooperative behaviour are all social goals relevant to schools and linked to learning outcomes. However, schools cannot hope to target social outcomes effectively unless they also measure them. This will provide some idea of what is actually occurring in their classrooms and playgrounds, what it is like for students attending and what the social issues are.

Some schools are beginning to conduct regular surveys that are extremely helpful in targeting social issues. In one city high school, students reported that over twenty-five percent of bullying occurred in classrooms where the teacher took no action. This could be because bullying was so much a part of normal classroom behaviour that the teachers didn't even see it. What is more, thirty percent of students felt that nothing could be done about the level of bullying.

Schools keep records of suspensions, expulsions, bullying (or other) incidents reported, as well as counsellor referrals, attendance and discipline records and the like, but these are narrow and negative measures of social competence. They do not provide a good picture of the social behaviour and skills acquired by students as a result of their schooling. The otherwise influential 1994 *NSW Parliamentary Report into Boys' Education* analysed educational outcomes for both boys and girls exclusively in terms of academic results and subject participation rates. It failed to include any meaningful measures of social outcomes.

Masculinity and sexuality

After working for some years as a sexuality educator, it is apparent to me that boys' notions of masculinity and male sexuality are closely linked and strongly reflect traditional male culture.

> *Much of the disruptive, hostile and aggressive behaviour*
> *expressed by boys occurs in groups where there is an audience.*
> *Many of these behaviours have a strong sexual component such*
> *as constant sexual references, calling each other 'poofters', and*
> *other forms of sexual harassment. It's my view that any strategy*
> *that takes account of masculinity and male behaviour will have*
> *to address sexuality issues, with boys in groups.*

On the positive side, I have found that by beginning with issues of sex and sexuality it is possible to establish sufficient group interest and safety to begin talking about issues of masculinity in the classroom. The smaller the group size the easier it is to discuss these issues. Not all groups are resistant. In one Year 10 boys-only program the boys asked, 'What took you so long?' (to start talking about these issues with us).

A related concern is the need for men to be involved in teaching aspects of sexuality to boys. I realised this when I noticed comments about boys going through puberty, such as, 'Poor Ben, he can't help himself. His hormones are going wild.' While these kind of remarks are said in a spirit of generosity and forgiveness, they also give certain messages to young boys about sexuality:

- Sexuality is out of your control.
- You can't control your behaviour.

This is very close to the idea that 'I'm not responsible for my behaviour', and in particular, too close to part of the rape myth that claims, 'I couldn't help myself. She led me on.' It also links to sexual harassment: 'Look at the way she's dressed. She was asking for it.'

It is necessary to give boys the message that although sexual development feels chaotic and their emotions may be unpredictable, there is no time when their sexual behaviour is out of their control. Sometimes when a woman attempts to convey or teach this point of view to boys, the challenge arises, 'Well, how would you know?' and 'Why is she telling us to control our sexual behaviour?' Men can convey this message with more credibility, having been through the experience of puberty as a male.

Apart from this area, albeit a significant one, it is not yet clear which topics are better taught to boys by men. What is important is that men are involved and role model the kinds of attitudes to masculinity and sexuality we want boys to develop. Such men certainly have to be at ease with their own sexuality. Ironically, it is women who have traditionally taught Personal Development to boys. Men must be involved so that it is no longer seen as 'women's work'. Personal Development is important enough for both men and women to take central roles.

The debate about boys' education, gender, violence, masculinity and the need to improve the social outcomes of schooling is here to stay. The need for change seems to be publicly accepted. Teachers that I know are relieved that the gender focus now includes all students. The next step is to make sense of the programs and initiatives that are working and see how we can extend and build on them across all schools.

The conclusion for me is that changes in boys' behaviour are a part of changes in the larger system and will frequently involve reassessing the use of power and authority. On top of that, learning – especially about gender and masculinity – is a function of the quality of relationships. Consequently, the deliberate building of better classroom and parent relationships is critical to improving both gender relations and learning outcomes.

Rollo Browne consults to schools on boys' education, masculinity and gender relations. He presents regularly at conferences and staff development seminars. Rollo began teaching in Aboriginal communities in the Northern Territory more than fifteen years ago. Returning to New South Wales, he became an educator with the Family Planning Association, developing programs such as 'Year 10 Boys and Masculinity' and the Cleveland Street Antihomophobia Seminars. Subsequently he worked with the Human Rights Commission in the areas of privacy, race and sex discrimination. He now has his own company, conducting a variety of manager-development programs in organisations.

Boys' team also does well

Can Media Studies classes be used to challenge the gender stereotypes held by boys of males? *Su Langker*, a teacher of Media Studies in Sydney, considers how one class took offence at the media portrayal of young men – and began to understand the wider implications of stereotyping for both genders.

was teaching a unit on Advertising to a Year 11 class. We had just completed an investigation of the way in which advertisements for scents, for both men and women, constructed images designed to sell a product that really cannot be properly described. How do you describe a smell?

The young women were all very interested in scent but at the end of the unit were quite angry – saying, 'How dare they treat us like that!'.

The boys, however, showed little emotional involvement in the exercise. This led me to wonder how young men would respond to similar examples of image manipulation.

'Hey, is this really you?'

I showed them 'Over half a million cool ones in every issue', an advertisement in B&T, a trade magazine designed for the advertising industry. This ad was selling to advertisers a particular audience – the readers of Street Machine (who included some boys in my class). The caption under the headline promised to deliver '566 000 mostly young, blue collar, male readers'. And then came their offer: 'So when you're ready for another half million potential

> *softdrink users, jeans and sneaker wearers, beer and spirit drinkers, lovers of snack foods and motor cars, call our advertising sales offices. And we'll deliver them in our Street Machine'.*

The students' response varied from disgust to resentment. Disgust was felt by the young men that – because they liked cars (and, yes, cars were an important part of their culture) – they should be seen as a job lot of morons bent on self-destruction. Resentment was felt by the young women (who also liked cars) that they weren't even included in the insult.

This became part of an investigation of how the mass media sells audiences to advertisers. By looking at various advertisements from advertising magazines we discovered that all types of males and females are neatly packaged for sale to advertisers. The pressure on males to succeed was discovered in the promise by *Australian Business* to deliver 'Twice the Chair*men*'. The need for males to be heroes, legends, champions (as perceived by advertising executives) was discovered in *Time* magazine's claim that it is the 'Breakfast of Champions', while *The Bulletin* put the pressure on males to uphold literary values with its promise to deliver 'More *Men* Of Letters'.

As the young men in my class didn't feel the pressure (very strongly) to be either chairmen or men of letters, their reaction to these advertisements was quite subdued. However the young women expressed resentment at being left out of the picture – perhaps because they had been exposed to more activities designed to make them question the status quo.

In the case of the young men, it took the *Street Machine* ad to get a response. Now they were presented with the depiction of the audience of a magazine they really liked – and I could say, 'Hey, is this really you?' This made them question the way they seemed to be expected to behave. There is nothing like a sense of being manipulated to initiate questioning of the validity of group behaviour.

From ethnic to gender stereotypes

> *As part of a Year 9 unit on stereotyping, we had 'deconstructed' and 'reconstructed' some advertisements using ethnic stereotypes. We rewrote an advertisement for a certain credit card using a stereotypically aggressive Greek man. The new ad now made fun*

*of an Anglo-Saxon stereotype – something to do with Austra-
lians and thongs and the inability to add up – much to the
delight of the class. Also we made a video poking fun at ethnic
stereotyping. Playing with gender stereotyping was the obvious
thing to do next.*

*Students were grouped into pairs, comprising 'talent' and
'director'. Each pair chose a colour print advertisement containing a clearly dominant model of either sex, ensuring it was the
opposite gender to that of their 'talent'.*

*The pose was studied, and the student who was the 'talent'
struck that pose while the 'director' checked that the eventual photograph would fit the one in the advertisement in all aspects.*

*The teacher photographed the 'talent' so that the result could be
cut and pasted over the original, completely deleting the model of
the opposite sex. In one case, it was noticed that a certain Swe-
dish furniture chain, to its shame, depicted the person who
changed the light globe as male, thus reinforcing the idea that
males do the dangerous work while admiring females look on. We
soon changed both those roles! The resulting posters were
proudly displayed in the school. The boys, in particular, were
quite proud of their modelling work.*

The very embodiment . . .

By considering male celebrities in film, rock music and sport, we
examined the way stars are constructed to show us how to be
male. We found that stars – especially those used in advertising
– presented different ideas on how to be male in different periods.

*From a 1950s advertisement for Club 'men's chocolate' (starring
Chips Rafferty) we learnt about what was expected of an Australian male in the Fifties. He had to have a 'tall, easy-going figure
and [a] soft drawl' and be 'the very embodiment of a typical
Australian'. This description was reinforced by a picture of this
star (of such rugged Australian films as* Eureka Stockade*) showing an Anglo-Saxon smiling face with moustache and broad-
brimmed hat. His favoured occupation was indicated by the
comment that the chocolate, 'cracks like a stockwhip'.*

At the time of our study, Jason Donovan was a popular star
in the soap opera 'Neighbours' and Grant Kenny a much-

publicised 'iron man' (or surf champion). It was, therefore, interesting to compare the media images of Jason Donovan and Grant Kenny (and what they were saying about how one should be male in the Eighties) to that of Chips Rafferty.

The main comment in class was that males were obviously (then and now) expected to be Anglo-Saxon. (Perhaps the realisation that no-one in our class was from that ethnic background was a factor!) As well as being Anglo-Saxon, the ideal Australian man in both eras was expected to represent all that was admirable in Australian culture. Grant Kenny's advertisements for the breakfast cereal Nutri-grain celebrated the glories of the Australian surf and its bronzed conqueror. The hero had moved from the outback to the surf but retained the idea of 'the very embodiment of a typical Australian'.

> *Jason Donovan, on the other hand, represented 'the boy next door'. He was the so-called all-Australian, white-skinned good-looking boy (who had trouble passing his Higher School Certificate). In our final classes the students created advertisements using stars whose value systems clashed completely with the image previously given to the product. One example was Boy George (a very different, English pop star who made a cult of cross-dressing) promoting Nutri-grain.*

Constructing an image

The English classes in our school were graded to create smaller classes and allow for more concentrated work on literacy in the lower range. As a result, most of the bottom classes consisted mainly of boys whose self-esteem (in relation to their work in English) was very low. They were particularly weak in producing work which was well laid out and attractively presented. This was obviously going to affect their employment prospects.

With one of these underachieving Year 11 classes we looked at the way the media presents young people. They began with a consideration of the images they presented, talking about such aspects as clothing, hairstyles and body language. Each student then created a personal profile – complete with a photograph and descriptions of their interests and abilities – designed to project the image they would like to have.

As the layout and presentation of this profile was very important to them (and seen as a practice for a curriculum vitae) their presentation skills improved as did their self-esteem in that area. This was important, as it was an area in which they thought only girls excelled. They realised, too, that image is something you construct for yourself and that one can change it if one so wishes.

Further development of their self-esteem occurred when groups of boys completed the task of producing magazines which ridiculed the various stereotypes (cultural, ethnic, sexual and physical) found in popular magazines for young people. Again, the boys had undertaken something quite ambitious (magazine production) in an area in which, usually, only girls excelled. This time it was the turn for the boys' self-esteem to rise as they handed in their beautifully produced magazines depicting all sorts of role-reversals.

Boys as sex objects

What happens when boys are asked to present themselves as sex objects? This issue arose when the boys were asked to provide the 'talent' (in the strict media sense) for a video which the girls were making (entitled Boys, Boys, Boys*). The boys had to consider role-reversal and how they would present themselves as sex objects.*

Many of them, of course, copied what they had seen in the media about how to be macho. *Others, perhaps more true to their local culture and ethnic background, chose to do a double-act with their cars – the car being an expression (or perhaps an exten-sion) of their own sexuality. We were treated to wonderful scenes of burning rubber as well as slow cruising down the main street.*

In talking about it afterwards, the young men said they posed as they did because they were heroes or because that was how the girls liked them. They appeared to have been quite correct in this assumption as the video clip became extremely popular at a neighbouring girls school and in their own school. It is probable that the young women gained more from the exercise (in the way of confidence and self-esteem) but at least it was talked about.

Boys' team also does well

Success with raising boys' self-esteem (in the area of writing through magazine production) led me to think about what could be done in a formal Journalism class. Our school newspaper, *No Frills*, was produced by a small group of volunteers during

Wednesday afternoon Sport. There were not very many boys involved. With the support of the school principal, I wrote a course for Year 9 Journalism which was also approved by the NSW Board of Studies. Now I had a class of mixed ability and mixed gender – certainly a challenge. A great deal of time was needed in one-to-one help with writing. However, soon some boys (who had previously seen English as an impossible subject in which only girls could do well) became very happy about their ability to contribute.

One boy in particular, who was barely literate, became (with guidance and the motivation of seeing his work in print) far more confident in his ability to write. Consequently, he improved markedly in English. Other boys became regular contributors to the paper's poetry page, which had began as very much the girls' domain.

> The newspaper also provided an opportunity to lessen some of the burden on the boys of having to uphold the sporting honour of the school on their own. When the school's indoor soccer team (made up of girls) became State champions, the headline on the sports page of No Frills read: 'Marrickville High Soccer Team State Champions'. In smaller type, lower on the page, was another head-line: 'Boys' Team Also Does Well'. The boys' team **had** done well, but not as well as the girls, contrary to what many people might have expected. This policy in sports reporting pleased both boys and girls, who saw it as the way things should be.

Young men are 'expendable'

After two years in an inner-city boys selective school, I realise how much easier it is to encourage boys to study the images of males in the media in the context of the images of females. In a coeducational school the girls set the pace, as they are usually all aware of female stereotyping.

I had been searching for an idea that might stir some concern in the boys about their manipulation by the media. We had been discussing a report in the *Sydney Morning Herald* on the recent Higher School Certificate results (emphasising the new superiority of girls' performances over the boys) when a chance conversation brought up the idea that young men are constantly seen as expendable. Suddenly everything seemed to support this idea and it seemed to be a useful strategy to explore.

A correspondent to the Sydney Morning Herald *pointed out that even in a toy stores catalogue, boys' and men's models have such names as 'Intimidator', 'Batman', 'Python', 'Shock'. On the other hand, the girls' and women's models are named 'Mystique', 'Sweetie', 'Mysty Magic' and 'Tres Chic'. The boys seem to be being encouraged to hurt others and, by implication, themselves. This suggests that while we encourage girls to take care of themselves, we, as a society, don't seem nearly as concerned to preserve our young men. As they grow older the boys seem to be encouraged to associate with images of war and fighting.*

This very concept could also be seen in an interesting article in B&T, *'Ray Bans gunning for new image'. The article provided the starting point for a new Media course I was introducing for Year 11. The campaign for Ray Ban sunglasses (designed to 'shake off its yuppie image') was selling war games to boys and wanted to cash in on the military background of the sunglasses. A ninety-second cinema advertisement took the viewer through a day in the urban jungle of New York, ending with the line, 'Ray Bans – designed for war zones' to the accompaniment of a gun shot. Print ads also played with military and tough images. One, for example, read: 'If they can survive Pearl Harbour, Korea and the Gulf, they'll survive your glove box'. Tag Heuer ('Don't crack under pressure') and Bollé also present a similarly tough image.*

The students began investigating the manner in which advertising (always ready to perpetuate the dominant ideologies of the time) supports and exploits the idea that young men are expendable. At first the young men in my class found this idea very amusing but then began looking for such advertisements themselves, bringing in magazines which contained advertisements which they thought encouraged young men to endanger their lives and take risks.

The message from the magazine

The magazines introduced into the class by the students suggested our next step. As these had been magazines designed for men, we decided to choose one and analyse it for evidence of encouragement to young men to self-destruct (or at least to accept others instructions to destroy themselves and others).

The magazine, Inside Sport, *was selected. It appeared to be a magazine intended, it would indeed seem, for young males. This conclusion was reached not just from an examination of the advertisements it contained (the usual way of determining an intended audience) but from the proportion of pages devoted to bikini-clad young women distinguished more by their pulchritude than their obvious sporting prowess. (We examined the issue for January, 1995.) Such photographs take up sixteen of the magazines 144 pages as well as the front cover. Although it could be argued that women might be interested in the pictures as fashion statements, the garments shown are neither practical for swimming nor particularly fashionable!*

What did the magazine contain? Of thirty-seven full-page advertisements, seventeen percent encouraged speed either in fast cars or water skis, with language which left no doubt that speed was exciting. Twenty-two percent of the advertisements were for alcohol, while forty percent encouraged ruggedness in clothes, watches or travel. Fearlessness was sold in five percent of the advertisements while health-related advertisements made up sixteen percent. Unlike those relating to health in women's magazines, these advertisements were for sports drinks for the rugged male or for sunscreens (which mostly projected the tough, sweat-resistant image, not ones for everyday, sensible use).

Mr Cleo meets Mr Inside Sport

Our subsequent discussions focused on why young men are seen as expendable and the possible reasons behind such encouragement. The students made the suggestion that as traditionally it was young men who were expected to fight wars, it was understandable that they should be encouraged to project a tough, dominant image and enjoy physical confrontation. Are these the only images of men to be found in magazines, they asked. One young man, Kevin, brought in some copies of *Cleo*. He pointed out that here we might find a very different image of men – and, of course, he was right. The men in *Cleo* were pictured with women and with families. They were caring, sensitive young people who liked clothing not so very different from that worn by women. The students decided to 'act out' *Mr Cleo* and *Mr Inside Sport*; I suggested they make a video in which the two would meet.

The video began with a series of soft-focus shots of males from
Cleo *and other women's magazines. These images faded into
each other and finally into our* Mr Cleo *in a similar pose. It cut
to a doctor's waiting room where our two heroes are reading magazines and become involved in a discussion about these, revealing
their attitudes to life and (particularly) women. As* Mr Inside
Sport *speaks, there is a fade to a series of shots of men from that
magazine. Their attitudes are further revealed in the way they
relate to the young woman who is the doctor. (There was, addi-
tionally, much interest in the style of man that she obviously preferred.) The video was scripted by one of the boys and directed,
filmed and acted by the others, so they were constantly discussing these conflicting images.*

Advertisers' stereotypes of men

Advertising for women often promotes a healthy lifestyle. (Consider the advertisements for meat, to provide sufficient iron in
the diet: 'If you're too tired to read this, you're exactly the sort
of person who should'.) The advertising industry has decided
that women are interested in their own health.

But what have advertisers decided about young men? We
looked at the products *Street Machine* hopes to advertise – soft
drink, beer, spirits, snack foods and motor cars. And where did
we find advertisements for healthy food? In *Street Machine*, in
Time, in the *Bulletin*? No, in *Women's Weekly* or *Woman's Day*.

The advertising industry is at last aware that much of its
advertising alienates women. The Affirmative Action Media
Awards (established by Women and Management Inc. with Nu-
Skin) acknowledge advertising which portrays women in
nonstereotypical ways. The boys were much amused by the
Affirmative Action Media Awards' advertisement in *B&T*, 'Will
the real Australian woman please stand up', showing a decidedly
unreal woman who could only be of interest to manufacturers of
'industrial strength hairspray'.

These students are now keen to get advertisers to think about
stereotypes of men as well. It will be interesting to see if an
advertisement asking, 'Will the real Australian man please stand
up?' ever appears in *B&T*.

Su Langker's interest in Media education began as a primary school librarian in the Seventies. This continued during her work at Catholic schools and through to her appointment to Marrickville High School, where she taught a Year 9 Journalism course, the subject, 'Understanding Television', to Year 11 and produced the school newspaper. Nowadays Su is teaching Year 11 Media at Sydney Boys High School. She has been very involved in teacher education, running in-services and conference workshops in Media.

Changing the lives of boys

Looking back at what has *not* changed since

his school-teaching days in the Seventies,

Richard Fletcher – a leading educator in the field of

male health – examines the difficulties schools face

with the behaviour and poor performance of

boys and considers some new initiatives

for change.

A flashback to 1971

8.45 a.m. Assembly.

I rocket my black 300 cc Honda motorbike into the teachers parking lot and grab the saddle bags. Dumping them with my leather jacket on my desk, I run quietly along the concrete and slide unobtrusively into the assembly being held in the quadrangle. Once in position, I take up my role. 'Abdulla, George,' I bark quietly to the boys punching another one in the back row of 3H. They look around nervously, then recover their cool and shrug their shoulders towards the podium at the front.

10.20 a.m. 3H comes into the lab.

'George. I'll have the cigarette lighter please.' Keeping control of who lights the bunsen burners is one of my basic strategies for survival – survival of the point of the lesson (the boys want to light the bunsens immediately and burn something), survival of the students (they are not above putting their ties in the flame for a dare) and my own survival as a teacher (the principal has spoken to me about rowdy classes: 'Inquiry learning is all very well, but if you can't control the class, you've got chaos, not learning'.)

George looks blankly at me while trying to palm the lighter. I take a step towards him. 'Give me the lighter.' I'm now using my 'I mean it' stare. My lips are stretched thinly and my face is (I hope) hard. I've decided if he doesn't hand it over I'll send him out to stand in the corridor. That's what I mean by 'serious'. If the deputy comes past on his regular corridor audit George will be up to the office for four cuts of the cane. If that happens, George will return to the class sullenly, he'll shoot me a poisonous look as he takes his seat but of course he will on no account look tearful or as if he is in pain. George hands over the lighter. 'Come and get it at the end of the lesson,' I say. This is a gesture of friendship. Cigarette lighters are banned in the school and teachers are supposed to confiscate them on sight. I don't, though, because snatching the students' lighters while we teachers puff away in the staff room seems too hypocritical.

11.10 a.m. Recess.

I can hear it before I get past the Library block, 'Fight, fight, fght, fight . . .' I round the corner and take a tense breath before moving into the milling circle of delighted boys roaring their chant at the two red-faced wrestlers rolling on the asphalt in a lather of blue shirts and missed punches. Reaching the fighters with some difficulty, I grab them by the shirt collars and haul them up. 'All right' I shout at the crowd, who are sensing their power and starting to boo. 'That's enough'. And I frogmarch the two up to the deputy's office for their reward, six of the best.

12.35 p.m. Lunch.

I'm on playground duty. I'm talking to Ashley, Diana and Cathy. 'Well, what about an industrial chemist?' I say, 'You're easily that smart.'

'We are not,' Diana responds.

'You could do it easily.' I laugh a genuine laugh. I know that these girls are bright. 'Do you think girls are really less intelligent than boys?' I taunt.

'Course not,' Diana says with conviction.

'Well, what could stop you being an industrial chemist?'

'Nah,' Cathy looks down, 'too smelly.' The others giggle.

'Checkouts aren't exactly perfume counters,' I reply.

'We're getting jobs at DJ's,' Cathy glances sideways at Diana. 'On the perfume counter,' Diana adds with perfect timing.

'It'll have to be a long counter,' I reply, trying to recover some ground, 'and you'll get varicose veins.'

2.20 p.m. A Year 5 Physics class.

'Will you get married?' I ask the fifth years in front of me. This is a relaxed group and they answer without a lot of self-consciousness. Almost everybody except the smart Alecs thinks they will, but the boys see it as a remote question. They've obviously never thought about it much. Pretty soon we're back into atomic theory.

3.30 p.m. Detention class.

I recognise three of the boys in the group. 'What are you in here for?' I ask.

'Miss Robertson,' Eric grimaces and looks away. Miss Robertson's history classes are famous for firm discipline.

'History for Hairy legs,' Boris mutters under his breath. I ignore this and tell them all – the twelve boys and the two girls – to get some homework out and start working.

Boris stands up immediately and approaches my desk with his bag. 'Mr Sanders said I gotta go to training.' He hands me a folded piece of school memo paper. 'Please excuse Boris from detention as he is required at football training today. Signed: G. Sanders.'

Too late to check. I nod, feeling outmanoeuvred and also undermined.

What's changed?

What's different in the 1990s? Judging from this excerpt, not much. At least, not as far as boys' behaviours are concerned. There is now some recognition of difference in learning approaches in our schools, especially for students from ethnic backgrounds. There is support for teachers and girls trying to avoid the narrow assumptions about girls' abilities. Feminist thinking – that girls deserve the same opportunities as boys – has become recognised as common sense. But we are still confused about directions for boys. It's true we don't cane boys these days, but we are some way from knowing how schools might serve boys well.

What is starting to change is our complacency about boys' behaviours and attitudes. We are also beginning to recognise that we don't know much about boys. This is not the same as discovering that boys are oppressed, just like girls, but it does mean noticing how poorly schools are serving boys. The recognition that boys are not 'the winners' in the contest for academic and social rewards is an important step.

Beyond the hype

Much of the recent media attention on boys has focused on the academic superiority of the girls. The 'news' is that suddenly, girls are getting ahead of boys in university entrance level exams. This has two unfortunate effects. It suggests that we are only concerned about the academic performance of the small percentage of boys who go on to university and, since the boys' poor showing is only recent, we should be able to fix it quickly.

But both of these suggestions are wrong. Of course the university entrance exams are important to those boys sitting for them, and their families. But in my view, the key issues for boys are wider than just tertiary entrance scores. Issues such as discipline, stereotyped content choice (e.g. English is for girls), and violence are vitally important for boys across the school spectrum and affect learning in all areas and at all levels.

> *A primary principal beckoned me into his office recently. 'Look at this,' he said. He was showing me the 'Time-out' book where pupils' names were recorded if they had been sent to the 'Time-out' room for discipline. He held the book open and flipped through the pages of names. 'Look, they are practically all boys!'*

The point is that there is absolutely nothing new about this situation. When I was teaching in the Seventies, detentions were full of boys. What is new is the realisation that boys being 'bad' is not just part of the natural order of things. Boys being uninterested in English, or being antisocial or slow readers is now being seen as a problem, not just by teachers but by parents and others concerned about education.

Boys' health

There are some parallels here between the areas of health and education. At the same time that boys' difficulties are being noticed in schools, health workers have been discovering that boys' health is not exactly wonderful. If we take the boys and girls in our primary schools as an example, while the deaths from diseases such as cancer will be about equal, twice as many boys will die from accidents such as falls and drownings as will girls. In high school, the road traffic accident rate worsens. And to that we have to add suicide, alcohol abuse and head injuries.

The concern from a health perspective is, quite clearly, not just with the boys in the top stream. It is the boys in the bottom classes of the school who are most likely to turn up in the morgues and casualty sections of the hospitals. Even though we have made impressive gains in health over the last twenty years, no-one thinks that we can just 'fix' boys' and men's behaviour.

Another reason to relate health outcomes to schooling is that the organisations of health and education are now becoming interlinked. For their part, schools have introduced a national curriculum in the area of Health. What was once a few sessions on hygiene, and 'PE' is now one of the eight key learning areas for all schoolchildren. From the health workers' side, they are recognising that many attitudes and behaviours are set in place during the school years (e.g. getting suntanned) which will later impact on health figures (skin cancer). National surveys reveal that twenty-nine percent of males in the fourteen to twenty-four age group are drinking on at least two days a week (compared to sixteen percent of females in this age group). And young males are particularly prone to binge drinking, that is, having five or more drinks in a row. By itself, this is an alarming figure for both sexes, but when it is coupled with the figures for boys' traffic fatalities (300 percent more than girls) and convictions for assault (700 percent more than girls) both of which are strongly related to alcohol abuse, the maleness of the problem becomes clear. Talking generally about *students* who drink or fight or drive recklessly is missing the point. Drinking, fighting and reckless driving all have a particular meaning for boys. They are important markers of manhood in our culture and strongly link health concerns to the need to re-examine boys' behaviour.

Health workers and school teachers are confronted by the same dilemma. How do we encourage boys into attitudes and behaviours which lead away from detention classes, casualty wards, morgues, detox units and jails?

The figures for boys' deaths, and the figures on detention rates, suspensions, literacy levels, behaviour problems and learning difficulties offer us an essential tool for thinking about boys. Addressing meetings of teachers and parents, I have found that in every case they are surprised to learn that boys aged up to fourteen die at significantly higher rates than girls, and that in the teenage years the gap widens. But what has the most impact is the picture of boys doing poorly across a whole spectrum of measures. Boys excel, not just at suicides, but at drownings, low literacy, drug offences, serious assaults, burns, language difficulties, spinal cord damage, sexual assaults, expulsions from school, alcohol abuse, reading difficulties, work injuries, attention deficit disorder and head injuries.

Looking at the outcomes in both academic and social areas has allowed teachers to see the advantages to be gained for boys if schools, and the boys, do change. This is an enormous step. Up until now, there have been just two competing views of boys in schools. The traditional view, that boys will just 'be boys', has meant that boys' difficulties have been considered too hard to change, or that these difficulties are part of being a man. On the other hand, when compared to the harassment of girls, boys' difficulties appear secondary. Neither of these approaches has helped figure out what to do with boys.

What's in it for boys?

As a high school teacher in the 1970s, I was beginning to see the potential benefit to be gained by women and girls from changes in schools. But I was completely at a loss with the boys. It did occur to me, while I was joking with Ashley, Diana and Kathy in the playground, that I would like to do the same with the boys. But how to achieve the same sort of light-hearted challenge with the boys? What could I say to them? That they could be industrial chemists? The boys in my top Science classes already saw themselves as future professionals. The lower stream boys were adamant that they'd be apprentices or at least hot rod drivers. As a group, the boys did seem to have more of everything. Overall, I knew, they were going to get the best jobs, and they would get to go to the pub and the footy. At the time I could not think of any positive way to suggest that boys change.

The beauty of using a wider range of outcomes (not just university entrance scores) to measure what schools do, is that it makes the whole project of gender equity more attractive. Change can benefit boys, not just take something away from them. And looking at health and social outcomes implies a broader idea of what we want for boys, not just a job and a car, but a life where values and relationships are important.

Starting out

Schools and parents are starting down this path – developing boy-friendly schools. But realistically, we are at the start of a long process. Some false starts are inevitable. One high school introduced a boys-only English class thinking that, since girls-only Science classes had raised the girls' performance, boys-only English might remedy the boys' abysmal English scores. The result was a disastrous classroom standoff between the frustrated teacher and the sullen boys who rebelled at doing a 'girls' subject. Recognising the long-term task ahead of us means accepting the need to think through the new approaches to boys.

The rush to 'fix boys up' comes not just from teachers, of course. A parent meeting to discuss boys at a Newcastle high school achieved a record attendance of more than 100 parents. After hearing about the wide range of problems faced by the boys, they wanted some action. A brief discussion led to one parent's suggestion – to have compulsory child care classes for all the boys. In this way she hoped to address boys' lack of understanding about parenting in a practical way, at the same time as encouraging the value of caring as opposed to competing. To my surprise, over half the parents present supported the idea, particularly the compulsory aspect. The principal quickly stepped in to point out the administrative implications of such a radical remedy and the meeting continued with a spirited debate. Those opposing the child care advocates were parents who saw it as their own job to pass on such skills and values.

The way this 'solution' was seized on by those present is a mark of the anxiety typically felt by parents (and many others) involved in the debate about boys. Not that the program suggested was without merit. On the contrary. Where this approach has been tried (albeit voluntarily) it has had surprising results. In the United States, 'problem boys' were offered a course in baby care with real live babies. Contrary to expectations, they loved it. The boys quickly became attached to the infants and rated their baby class the high point of the school week. When it was offered to the whole school the following term there was a long waiting list of boys wanting to do the class.

Nevertheless, as 'the solution', this suggestion is far too narrow. No one area – not curriculum, not playground rules, not teacher attitudes nor parental involvement – will by itself be sufficient. The issues for boys span the whole school environment and beyond, into the community, especially community-school relations. On the other hand, the good news is that it doesn't matter where schools begin. Whichever point they choose, other aspects of schooling will, after a time, require attention too.

However, one guiding rule for these initiatives is possible. As long as the boys' behaviours and the boys themselves are seen simply as problems – violent boys, disruptive boys, trouble-makers, the dominant group or whatever, then the programs developed to 'fix' them will end up as policing operations. Unless we truly want our schools to become prisons with more and more discipline for boys, we will have to link the values we wish to teach with valuing the boys themselves.

Valuing men and boys

One approach is for schools and parents to formulate a picture of what sorts of men we want our boys to grow into. The newness of this idea, of a positive picture of where boys are heading, can be seen when male teachers try to answer one simple question, 'What are you proud of about being a man?'

This question is asked as part of a School Staff Workshop which I have given for many high schools who request an introduction to Boys' Education. Before the workshop, I arrange with the school to have four or five male staff 'volunteer'. They are told that they will be asked, during the presentation, to come to the front (usually there are seventy or eighty staff) and answer some questions. This arrangement is to ensure that a cross-section of men give their views, such as the football coach or the industrial arts teacher as well as the agreeable young geography teacher who is happy to risk embarrassment out the front.

What do they answer? The first comment is almost invariably, 'Gee, I've never thought about it that much'. The rest of the men in the audience usually give a sympathetic laugh when they hear the question. Of course, the volunteers do go on to list qualities that they are pleased about or proud of. Physical strength and agility are common answers, as are the freedom to walk alone at night or to go bare-chested. Fatherhood is mentioned too. Some, though, find the question meaningless or can't think of anything, reflecting the traditional view that boys will automatically grow up into men. The point of asking the question is not in any way to denigrate the volunteers (they always get a round of genuine applause when they finish answering) but to raise the issue of what schools might value about boys. The men's reaction, and the staff discussion afterwards however, do make the point that thinking about what sort of men we would most like to see is a new question for schools, and that valuing boys is an important starting point in developing boys' education.

The issue of boys as future parents has one more important feature. It brings the interests of teachers and parents together most strongly. Teachers are in a very real sense *in loco parentis*, not just legally, but emotionally. If anything stands out when interviewing teachers about their concerns and hopes for boys, it is the depth of their wanting the best for their students. Daily life in schools, as in other big institutions, revolves around getting tasks done on time and within the rules. But beneath the banter and barking and information-giving, teachers want the boys (and girls) they teach to have rich, rewarding lives. The task of improving boys' schooling, and boys' lives, and thereby the lives of those they interact with, is certainly a challenge. But it is one which offers schools and parents an exciting chance to work differently together to define and encourage boys to travel down new paths.

Richard Fletcher taught Science in coeducational and all-boy high schools in Australia and overseas. In his subsequent work with the Health Promotion Unit in Newcastle, he pioneered the development of Men's Health and Boys' Health as areas of study. In 1992 he founded a community-based group, Fathers Against Rape, which conducted 'Stopping Rape' workshops with teenage boys in schools. He is a nationally recognised spokesperson on male health issues. As a lecturer in Health Studies in the Discipline of Paediatrics, University of Newcastle, he teaches Male Health Studies to nurses, trainee teachers, occupational therapists and medical students.

Nurturing boys, developing skills

Peter Ireland, Campus Principal of MacKillop Senior College at Port Macquarie, describes how his efforts to reach the 'uninvolved' majority of boys led to a successful initiative which engaged boys in the broader life of the school.

In my role as a teacher of teen-age boys in a senior coeducational college, I have frequently witnessed a lack of initiative and inhibited communication skills among the boys. Recently I overheard one parent say: 'My son seems content to cruise through life doing just enough to be left alone and to be seldom singled out for either responsibility or reprimand'. 'Yes,' another parent agreed: 'The boys enjoy being in a "comfort zone".'

Ex-students have also talked about their willingness to become involved in co-curricular activities while at school. Typical of the girls' comments were: 'I'm glad I had a go at things like debating while I was at school because it's been so useful at university and work ever since'.

However, I detected evidence of some regret in the comments from our male ex-students as they reflected on their senior school days: 'I wish I'd had a go at those things at school because I could have *really* used it now!'

These incidents add up to a picture of boys who are missing out on important aspects of school life, not from lack of opportunity, but from a lack of motivation.

Another aspect of this dilemma is suggested in this mother's comment: 'My son sits on things . . . he bottles them up inside. I don't know what he's thinking. Sometimes I couldn't tell whether he's happy, content, worried or just indifferent to us all at home. What can I do?'

This reminded me of something I once heard Rolf Harris say on TV when I was a teenager. He was being interviewed not long after his father had died. He began to cry and say how much he wished he could express his emotions more readily even now as a man. He publicly lamented the fact that he had never said 'I love you, Dad' to his father. He felt it and knew it but just couldn't express it and was sending a message out on TV to urge all young men to get over that hurdle and reveal their feelings – not just their tempers – but their tenderness as well.

To me, these stories point to the need for positive male role models if teenage boys are to enjoy adequate masculine development.

Boys' involvement in skill-building experiences – a background

Females have new expectations of young men today. There is no longer a place for the 'strong silent type'. Today, women want men to be articulate, sensitive, tender and compassionate, both in the workplace and in relationships. Young men today need to be good communicators in more than just a professional capacity. Traditional fathers are not well equipped to model these qualities to their sons. This leaves the sons underfathered.

If the father–son relationship exists only through playing sport and having a beer together, then our sons are being under-fathered. In a sense, this only supports a culture of toughness and lonely self-reliance, and of driving ambition which tends to focus on power – not gender equity or meaningful relationships. It is this sense of abandonment which Peter Carey develops as a theme in some of his successful books such as *Oscar and Lucinda* (Booker Prize winner 1988) and *Illywhacker*. The point I'm making is that as parents we must realise that young men (our teenagers) need relationships with other men – including their fathers – in deep and significant ways which go far beyond the sporting field or having a drink together. The narrow male stereotype (sometimes encountered in schools, legal systems, the corporate world and peer groups) tends to produce sons who are 'underfathered'.

If this is allowed to go unarrested, it will produce young men who are, literally, dying inside emotionally; young men who cannot reveal tenderness, weakness or longing – even to girlfriends, mothers or wives – let alone articulate it for their own good.

Against this background my heightened interest gave me a good reason to actively raise the profile of teenage boys in our college. To get it right, parents need to work with teachers, and help bring about an attitudinal change which will see our teenage boys join in and get the most out of all developmental opportunities so that they don't short-change their great potential.

Selecting the boys

To commence the project, I targeted three Year 11 boys. My criteria for selecting these three boys was simple: I wanted to work with an average type of student – not a 'high-flyer' who already had significant roles to play at the college. Each would need to be in my Year 12 Economics class the following year (1995) so that if the project continued, I could ensure daily contact with each of them. As far as possible, I wanted boys from different friendship groups.

I had decided to select only three boys for the reason that this would be more manageable for me. In my position of campus principal I am often besieged during lunch hours by the many 'unpredictables' which invade my time wandering the court-yards. By having only three students to gather in meant that it would be easier to get together more often. Besides, I wanted to make it work. Taking a whole class group may have been too ambitious and may have prevented a good idea from working well. In addition an important aspect of my project was to make regular contact either written, phone or face to face with each of the boys' parents. Their input and partnership in the project was essential, but more than three could have been unwieldy.

The first meetings

Initially, we met on the courtyard lawn in lunch hours. This had two effects. It captured the curiosity of those students who watched from a distance and wondered what we were talking about. It also made me, the campus principal, meet the boys relaxed on their territory. My office could have been too formal for what we were going to discuss and plan.

At the first meeting I asked Luke, Wade and Joel to be volunteers for specific activities or roles around the college as things came up. As soon as one of them said, 'Let's give it a go', I knew we were off and running. Such a reaction made me realise that although they were aware of the possible embarrassment factor, they still enjoyed the prospect that I was interested enough to choose them as trial candidates. (This was a positive side-effect already!) I could see that the venture had their interest. I was glad to hear one of their comments about our joint project as: 'Discovering more about what I'm not good at, then improving it'.

In the beginning I had felt the need to prepare some form of agenda, but the casual nature of our meeting changed all that. We had a goal in common and a good working relationship emerged. Despite the initial 'self-consciousness factor' they all had, each responded with a greater willingness each fortnight.

Twilight meetings with mums and dads

Not long after choosing the three boys, I contacted each of their parents to let them know about the venture and ask for their support. I was encouraged to continue with the project by some of the parents' comments at our first twilight get-together.

> Parent 1: *This will be great for him because he is used to sitting back on the sideline and letting his three younger sisters take the front stage in most things. If he can gain more confidence he might show more of a lead and initiative.*

> Parent 2: *This will be good for him because he tends to be shy and gets embarrassed easily if he is asked to do something in front of a group. This might help him push through that barrier.*

> Parent 3: *This might be good for him. I'm pleased he's been chosen because he has lots of ability but only does what he has to do – the bare minimum.*

Some of the other twilight meetings with parents involved devising new strategies for skill-building at home; making a comparison with the girls' level of involvement; and planning for a parent–son workshop on next year's college calendar.

Redefining masculinity

I sent an article home with the boys and asked each parent and son to write me their thoughts as a response. The article, 'Redefining Masculinity', stated that boys and men are acting out a role – often living a pretence – but inside are really victims of loneliness, compulsive competition and emotional timidity. This produced several interesting and thoughtful replies, including:

Parent: *Opportunities for men and women are great, but it's the mind and attitude that controls the result. In other words, the chances to experience something new and improve skills are everywhere. We've just got to want to do it badly enough.*

Student: *I think that many men are confused with the changing roles they are beginning to play. They are still used to a traditional male stereotype and are finding it difficult to come to grips with the 'SNAG' image. If men and boys are to overcome these problems, they are going to have to accept and begin understanding the views of others.*

Parent: *I would like to know more about the 'underfathered' concept.*

Parent (father): *Yes, I can identify with everything . . . the 'I'm fine, everything is OK, . . . I'm quietly desperate but just toughing it out' syndrome.*

Student: *Just as women get on with life and don't give in when things get too hard, men should be encouraged to do the same. There's more in it for us by giving of ourselves than by sitting back on the take all the time.*

Extracurriculum involvement – boys and girls

The boys were keen to get started on something. During one of our courtyard meetings we agreed to conduct a survey within the college. They drew up a list of all the established extracurricular activities that took place. Each of them decided to talk with the coordinators and identify the level of involvement of male and female students in these skill-building activities around the college. The results more than surprised us – in fact they were alarming!

1. Young Achievers Australia Scheme (90% female)
2. School Council (50%/50% but more female initiative at meetings)
3. Fundraising for charities (80% female)
4. Mock Trial Representative Team (90% female)
5. College Debating Team (100% female)
6. Public Speaking competitions – Lions, Rotary, Toastmasters (100% female)
7. College Choir group (90% female)
8. Literary competition (80% female)
9. Use of Library in lunch hours (70% female)
10. Volunteers for liturgies (80% female)
11. Canteen service duties (90% female)
12. College ceremonies – Anzac, Farewell, Graduation (60% female)
13. Creative and Performing Arts Festival (70% female)
14. Duke of Edinburgh Award Scheme (80% female)
15. Exchange programs (80% female)
16. Part-time work (70% female)

Academic achievement

The boys' underrepresentation in each of these areas made us think perhaps that the boys were concentrating only on academic study. So we examined the recent Higher School Certificate results lists. These would give, we thought, a measurable indicator of gender-based academic achievement. The boys were once again surprised. The figures showed significant success rates in favour of the girls. For example, in 1994, our female students scored an average of eleven points more than our male students in Tertiary Entrance Ranks – 70.00 for the girls against 58.4 for the boys.

We found the girls outperformed the boys by a significant amount in the majority of courses. In the forty Board of Studies courses offered at the college, the girls occupied first position in twenty-three of them. In fact, Luke, Joel and Wade were also surprised to discover that girls occupied the first, second and third places in nineteen courses out of forty, and in fifteen courses girls occupied the top six places.

Speaking about the lopsided survey results, one of the boys commented that senior boys at this age were happy to take an insignificant and background role at best. 'Leave it to the girls' the boys would say to themselves. The irony is that the girls do it – seize the opportunity and grow further by the experience (skilling) – while the boys lose out. In fact, the majority of boys seem happy to be out of the limelight when it comes to these activities both in and out of the classrooms.

Boys – sitting on the sideline

This led us to another discussion. At one of the next courtyard get-togethers, the boys and I resolved to brainstorm a few possible reasons behind boys' reluctance to take up opportunities provided to them each week. We had to be very honest with ourselves, even in our small group of four; stating an opinion sometimes meant taking a risk and exposing a self-perceived weakness. By taking turns to speak, the boys identified several reasons.

First, it seems that it's too tempting to take the 'soft' and 'lazy' option when it comes to volunteering or nominating for a public-speaking competition or school-service position.

Their second reason claimed that there exists a degree of insecurity, low confidence and low self-esteem among the boys when it comes to nominating for activities.

Third, one of them suggested that there is a lack of acceptable role models (fathers, teachers and older brothers) from whom to take a lead.

Fourth, they recognised some peer pressure within their year group working against involvement in extracurricular and some classroom activities. They suggested that some of this could be because 'relative to girls at this age, we are still physically and emotionally immature'.

Another reason they put forward was that, 'The girls are even more focused these days at school and college, because they realise that they will have to look after their own financial futures'. To this one of the boys added: 'Perhaps the "public" struggle females have had to face and engage in for recognition, credibility and equal opportunities has really been fought more vigorously, and more successfully in the minds and hearts of girls. If we (men) are to change, the same thing must happen to us.'

As we ended our brainstorming session, one of the boys summarised it saying: 'Our Years 11 and 12 male students appear to run second [to the girls] when it comes to initiative, resourcefulness, willingness to try something new, self-belief and autonomy, aspiration and interest, commitment, openness in communication, and a satisfaction with self and feeling of worth'. They all resolved to make a personal contribution towards enhancing their participation and skills.

Did things change?

As I began to work with the boys, I was encouraged by other staff members. They offered suggestions on how to include boys to a greater extent in events and activities. We eventually had the following key personnel working towards involving the boys in new opportunities:

1. The Year 11 year adviser began to offer the boys chances to participate.
2. Our Religious Education coordinator enlisted the boys' assistance for whole-school and Year 11 Liturgies.
3. The SRC coordinator invited the boys to participate and organise theme days and fundraising;
4. The sportsmaster encouraged their involvement and management of subsequent lunchtime and College Representative competitions.
5. Each of the boys' Pastoral/Home Room teachers used them for positions of responsibility and duties within their Pastoral group.
6. The college secretary enlisted the boys to welcome official visitors at the front office.
7. A boys' sssembly was run to focus attention on opportunities for the taking.

From chances provided by these staff members, it was encouraging to watch each of the three boys steadily search for extra ways to get involved and practise skills. They all acted competently as ushers for the Year 12 graduation ball and prizegiving. Each had a turn at chairing a full college assembly. This meant preparing and leading the community prayer as well as organising assembly agenda items. (They rehearsed this process with me first.) The boys also took active roles in the end-of-year farewell assembly as well as taking charge of equipment collection and storage. One of the most pleasing outcomes was to nominate themselves to stand for election to the student representative council. Two of the three were later selected from the shortlist of councillors by college staff due to their impressive showing over the second half of the year. Another example of the boys' volunteering was their readiness to take lead roles in the annual Year 11 Reflection Day.

Overall, the three boys have grown measurably in confidence, self-esteem, leadership, oral communication and commitment. Other students are now seeing positive role models. Staff are encouraging the students and have identified attitudinal changes. The parents are delighted.

Another great side-effect was other boys asking whether they might be included. This project was leading the way for other boys to participate in skill-building experiences. In other words, participation was gaining acceptance. In the second semester there were improvements not only in Luke, Joel and Wade, but also in other boys who wanted to share their success.

Conclusion

As a senior campus principal, many parents come to me with a concern that their sons are undergoing change. As Bryce Courtney wrote in his book, *April Fools Day*:

> *I discovered with all my sons that one morning they wake up and their world had changed. Instead of being happy kids they are morose and silent. Instead of quite liking their parents they now see them as practically mentally retarded . . . Everything 'sucks' . . . their anger, confusion, malice, ill-temper, thoughtfulness and superiority comes out in the form of locked arms across their chests and brows deeply furrowed . . . their voices drop an octave and they temporarily lose their ability to speak, this faculty being replaced with a Neanderthal grunt which covers every possible situation they may confront . . .*

Teachers are often faced with this as well. I often meet those 'concerned' parents years later and they gladly tell me 'everything is fine'.

Bryce Courtney captured this relief as well:

> *Then he suddenly kisses you for the first time in three years. Then he starts to chat and laugh as though nothing untoward has taken place in the preceding thirty-six months . . . the very idea of you as his mortal enemy . . . is now a preposterous*

thought, an invention of your own over-imaginative mind . . .
He even manages to say 'I love you Dad' . . . And the little shit
is instantly forgiven by his mother, who has been communicating
with him via his brothers for the last umpteen months. She hugs
him, bursts into tears of gratitude and asks him joyously what
he'd like for dinner . . .

This sounds like a happy ending. Parents from the Fifties, Sixties and Seventies could read and identify with it. So can I. But it's not the answer. For our boys, the sons of the Nineties, it is no longer enough just to get through. Even if boys rediscover mainstream life, as they will, in the 1990s we have to do more. Sure, inevitably they will get through the difficult teenage years but they could easily be just like their fathers were before them. This is not enough. It only perpetuates underfathering. During these teenage years parents still have to keep chipping away to get the message across that more is and will be expected of their sons in the way they communicate within relationships and in the workplace. They need all the practice they can get at this by becoming more active in the school community.

I encourage all parents to use a recipe which is positive and optimistic. Don't get caught up in the doom-and-gloom brigade. The Nineties are full of hope and new possibilities. Good parenting and teaching can do much to nurture the soul and psyche of a sensitive and developing teenage boy.

Peter Ireland has taught in Independent and Catholic secondary schools for sixteen years. He is currently Campus Principal at MacKillop Senior College in Port Macquarie, New South Wales. His areas of interest include offering students skill-building experiences to enhance self-esteem and assisting boys, specifically, in becoming better verbal communicators in school classrooms, relationships and families. With his wife, Shirley, Peter is a parent to four children (Sally, Hannah, John and Bede).

Schools and the construction of masculinity

One way to gain insight into the behaviour of boys
is by considering how society, in all areas, shapes
acceptable masculine behaviour. *Rollo Browne,*
an independent consultant in boys' education,
shows how schools can play a vital part in
challenging and reshaping
boys' understanding and
experience of masculinity.

I t is in schools, during the formative years, that notions of masculinity (so often linked to such images as strength, cleverness, winning, power and status) are reinforced daily. Schools are a potent site for young people to absorb messages about what it means to be male and female. As parents and teachers become more aware of the wider social issues of boys' attitudes and behaviour, they are asking, 'Where do we begin with boys and masculinity? How can we make a difference?'

Social needs and the gender regime

The first step is to consider how boys see their needs and how they get them met.

Each person has a set of social needs that can only be met through relating to others. We have all seen the intensity of boys poring over basketball cards, computers, hot-rod photos or football magazines. When they are involved in these activities, with other boys in their group, some of their social needs are being met. These include the need for belonging, attention, physical closeness, being valued and using their imagination. This drive to get social needs met is a continuous part of their lives at school – and elsewhere.

> *Simon, a thirteen-year-old, glues near-naked models into his folder. He picks the time to display them for maximum effect. It makes a big difference who is around. If his English teacher, Mrs Jutter, a stickler for behaviour, sees it she might go off her brain – there is a school rule against sexist posters. If some girls come past while the boys are clustering around Simon, and he makes comments on their breast size and bodies, then he may even gain some status from his peers. At the same time Simon is attracted to Sharin, and if she comes into the classroom and sees what's going on, she's likely to think he's a jerk. When she is around he acts differently.*

From an early age we have all learned from experience to closely observe the kinds of behaviours that, as males and females, are likely to get our social needs met. Boys have learned the range of support or criticism they will get for behaving in particular ways: admitting to being hurt, dobbing someone in, swearing at other boys. Touching, for example, brings out strong reactions in high schools – boys with their arms around each others' shoulders typically get abused as 'poofters'. In Simon's case, perving at women's bodies is one way of showing his growing sexual identity and of getting into a group with other boys.

The actual behaviour that a boy like Simon chooses depends very much on who is present and what kind of supports or restraints apply. The balance of supports and restraints determines how successful his behaviour will be in getting his social needs met. It also establishes what behaviour is and is not acceptable as a male. Taken as a whole, the network of supports and restraints makes up what is called a 'gender regime'. There are many aspects to this. The school gender regime includes such things as: the way the school is organised; how power is used; the kind of school policies in place; the gender balance of executive positions, staff composition and staff dynamics; the teaching methods used; the kinds of subjects offered; the relations between staff and students, and so on. It is within such a gender culture that boys learn how they, as males, should behave to get their social needs met.

This information is absorbed constantly by students, and they use it in deciding how they are going to behave. These decisions can occur very fast and without much forethought at all. If a particular behaviour works they are likely to try it again.

Successful role models and dominant forms of masculinity

There are two other important influences on how boys behave: successful role models in the school and the dominant cultural forms of masculinity in society.

Boys are keenly aware of each other's behaviour, particularly the behaviour of those students with some sort of status in the school – how they dress, how they act. These 'cool guys' model apparently successful ways of getting social needs met. That is, their behaviour at least *looks* successful. Role models are likely to include school sports figures, local heroes or those students who hate school and seem to get many of their social needs met anyway. Certain teachers may also be role models – perhaps those who always get their way (by bullying students) or those teachers who have built positive relations with students.

The dominant cultural forms of masculinity in society are made up of the beliefs and stereotypes about being male that are most widely accepted. Boys are well aware of the roles of men at home, in the community, in business and in national affairs. Men are seen as a socially privileged group – as the breadwinners, decision-makers, risk-takers, power-brokers and as having had access to a wider range of opportunities, education and jobs than women. These images are well known through the effects of the media and of advertising. Movie stars, such as Arnold Schwarzenegger and Jean-Claude van Damme (a kick-boxer), embody notions of power, violence and justice to which many boys aspire. Often these dominant forms of masculinity and femininity are assumed to be the natural characteristics of each sex. Some examples might be that girls are nurturing and not aggressive; that boys are insensitive and status oriented.

In putting these elements together, as shown in Figure 1 over the page, we can build a picture of how a boy makes sense of his behaviour as a male and how he constructs his view of masculinity.

In working with masculinity and gender, the issues seem so interwoven that it is difficult to know where to start. In every school, it is as if there is a web of interconnected influences and pressures: for example; the curriculum, assessment procedures, teacher interventions, school structure, peer relations, staff relations, teaching methods, discipline and welfare. When you push one part of the web the whole structure flexes and absorbs the disturbance. In one sense, as in a circle, there is no particular starting point. The advantage of this is that schools can start where there is the most energy available. However it becomes obvious that changes at any one point will not generate any overall momentum until a number of related policies and practices are in place.

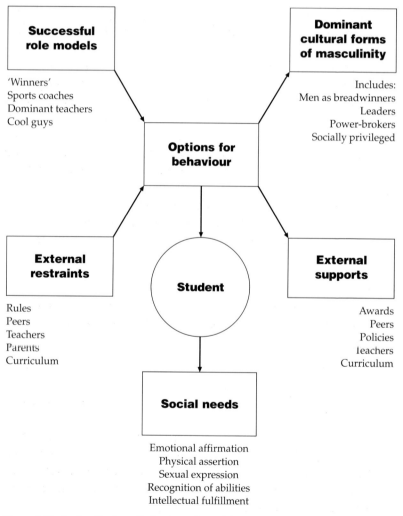

Figure 1: Understanding boys' behaviour: the social construction of masculinity

It is also a mistake to focus on any single element – for example, to only teach about stereotypes. Boys' education initiatives – in fact all gender-equity programs – require more than this. Stereotypes are only a part of the picture. As a theory, the social construction of masculinity is dynamic and subtle in its complexity. Our response needs to be equally broad.

Intervention points

So, how do we influence the web of gender relations in a school? One way is to apply the framework from Figure 1 to help us consider how to intervene in the social construction of masculinity at the school.

A school can look at each area in the model and work out what elements need to be changed, reinforced or challenged in terms of its role in relation to social needs, the network of supports and restraints for boys' behaviours (the gender regime of the school), successful role models and dominant forms of masculinity. In this way, sufficient challenges may be made to the existing school system for boys to reconsider their options for behaviour and what it means to be male.

The following list of suggestions includes initiatives being taken in schools. The list is not prescriptive or exhaustive, and some ideas may overlap. You may have other suggestions of your own.

Social needs

The school can examine its aims and current performance in this area. 'What do we want to teach boys about social needs?', 'Do we have programs that achieve any of the points below?':

- Legitimise feelings and build emotional literacy (ability to recognise and name feelings).
- Develop expression and communication skills (especially listening).
- Manage anger, teach recognition of the physical cues that precede an outburst. (The experience of the Aggression Replacement Training curriculum shows that social skills must be combined with both anger management and moral reasoning [thinking skills] to be effective.)
- Develop awareness of gender construction.

- Make good information on sexuality issues available at appropriate times. (By the end of Year 5, many students have already developed attitudes about sex, prostitution, homosexuality, etc.)
- Teach the difference between assertiveness and aggression.

External restraints

- Develop a clear discipline policy, linked to student welfare, focusing on the notion that the student takes responsibility for his behaviour as opposed to having the right to attend class regardless of his attitude to learning. This requires regular in-servicing of students and new staff on the policy. (See the chapter on discipline and welfare 'Give me a helmet' by Fred Carosi and Ross Tindale.) Linked to this would be consistent approaches to aggression and bullying (e.g., Pikas' no-blame method for bullying incidents) and school policies specifically targeting all forms of harassment and discrimination. (See the chapter on bullying, 'Cowering behind the bushes', by Coosje Griffiths.)
- Reduce corridor movement. One high school noticed much less disturbance in the corridors when the school day was reduced from eight to four periods.
- Challenge the peer culture. This ranges from teachers intervening in classroom abuse to running topics related to such issues as homophobia, violence and bullying, and power. (See 'Can I use the word "gay"?' by Maria Pallotta–Chiarolli.) In relation to violence and bullying, teach students to recognise what is and is not violence, to use conflict-resolution techniques (particularly in peer mediation) and to get bystanders to intervene in instances of bullying. In relation to power, introduce explicit teaching about the use and abuse of power. Teach that there are ways of being powerful other than *power over* others. Address the 'cool to be a fool' ethic.
- Involve the parent body (especially fathers) as well as the wider community. (As an example, see Richard Fletcher's chapter, 'Looking to fathers', which discusses the Fathers Against Rape initiative in Newcastle.) Community involvement is particularly relevant where students are from cultures that treat women as inferior to men.

External supports

- Adjust the use of power within the school so that it is not primarily punitive. One focus would be to raise the quality of teacher interventions in difficult situations. These are the critical moments where teachers model how adults get their needs met and exert control. Teachers may be using put-downs or colluding with homophobia and harassment or bullying to do this. Suitable role modelling by male teachers is important – in particular, men running sexuality programs for boys.

- Introduce on-site professional development to break down teacher isolation, using structured peer-feedback to get teachers to question and reflect on the effects of what they do in their classrooms. (See my chapter, 'Power and Classroom Relations'.)

- Develop policies to support individuals subjected to harassment, including clear grievance outlines. Introduce initiatives for your school to become a 'telling' school.

- Use merit and award systems to reward positive behaviour change. Assembly times often promote sport over other achievements. In one city high school, their two-dollar merit vouchers for the school canteen are surprisingly popular. One country high school gives merit points that can be converted into discounts at the local shops. At another school a highly valued prize was the opportunity for the student and his parents to be served tea and cake in the principal's office.

- Raise the profile of the expressive arts – Art, Drama, Music, Dance, etc. One primary deputy commented that he was now in the least violent school of his career. He put this down to the most active Music and Drama program he had ever seen. The boys who wanted to be cool were inside rehearsing. One indicator of a school making progress can be the amount of poetry by boys being published in the school magazine.

- Use positive classroom techniques (such as cooperative learning) to build classroom relationships and strategies that include different learning styles. Engage students in discussions of how they learn best and work out how to structure lessons to the students' advantage. This is also relevant for schools moving to a four-period day as different teaching techniques will be required. One teacher of Year 8 lower-stream students found that when she began 'creating' reasons to let a couple of boys walk around the classroom every so often during the lesson, the level of disruption dropped significantly.

- Further develop peer-support systems (to improve relations across year levels), conflict-resolution skills and peer mediation programs. This may involve making students part of the pastoral care system.
- Increase student influence over day-to-day activities. Most importantly, the issue of increased subject choice for students. When students have more say over what they learn they are less resistant to classes. A minor but significant issue is adoption of student-designed uniforms. Students in one city high school designed a bomber jacket in the school colours and it became a fashion item. The number of students who regularly wore the school uniform increased.
- Institute some executive-accountability structures for gender-equity programs. Hold separate boys activities where appropriate.
- Use surveys to collect information on student perceptions about school, conflict, bullying, which subjects they prefer and why, territoriality in the playground and so on. This can be used as a basis for policy review or lessons.

Successful role models

This is probably the hardest part of the framework to change. A change in role models is more likely to be an indicator that other changes are working. Some ways of redefining successful role models might include the following:
- Use assembly time to show alternative forms of success.
- Ensure teachers (as role models) display effective (and acceptable) ways of how adults get their needs met.
- Introduce collaborative or cooperative use of power within the school structure, and involve the parents and the wider community (*power with* versus *power over*).

Dominant forms of masculinity

Challenges to dominant forms of masculinity might include some of the following:
- Examine (in Media Studies) the messages that are embedded in TV programs, films and advertising. This is particularly important at junior levels. (See the chapter 'Boys' team also does well' by Su Langker.)

- Challenge gender stereotypes and images across the curriculum. (See the chapters: 'Breaking the rules', on Drama by Kathy Kokoris; 'It's not the way guys think!', on English by Wayne Martino; and 'The worst class in school?', on History by Allen Littlewood.)
- Focus on your school's Girls' Education Strategy. By its existence it challenges the status quo – for example, access to equipment, playground areas, computer time and single-sex classes.
- Provoke discussion of wider choices in subjects for boys. One school wanted all boys to do a unit in child care.

Options for behaviour

Boys reassess their options for behaviour when they have experienced alternative ways of getting their needs met. Suitable opportunities for boys to develop such awareness can come through schools running mentor-relationship schemes and small group programs for boys. (See the chapter on primary programs by Peter Clarke and the chapter on mentoring by Peter Ireland.)

The range of activities is as large as the number of issues to consider. When reflecting on where your school might begin, it is essential to ask where the staff as a whole would most benefit. Usually this is where they have the most investment in making changes and are most likely to carry them through consistently.

It is also important that the good work being done in one area is not wasted because it is not sufficiently supported by what other teachers are doing. Often, programs such as a Year 7 Boys Day or a topic on gender issues in Year 11 Drama remain one-off isolated instances, dependent on the energy of the individual teachers or parents.

As teachers and parents, we need to address the way masculinity is shaped at schools. What has been missing is a coherent approach to understanding how the school as a system reinforces gendered behaviour and therefore how to deliver positive change. There is no single 'right' way for a school to meet these challenges. Nor is it possible to guarantee the outcomes or know in advance the most effective ways to influence the social construction of masculinity across the education system. This chapter represents a first step in a long-term process of implementation and follow-through. We will only know the path by walking it.

Notes

Introduction

Rollo Browne can be contacted at P O Box 1042, Rozelle, NSW 2039 and by phone on (02) 555 8424.

Richard Fletcher can be reached at the Faculty of Medicine and Health Sciences, University of Newcastle, NSW 2308 and by phone on (049) 216 401.

In relation to Richard Fletcher's introduction, *Boys health measures* (both as boys and as future men) are discussed in the following publications: Fletcher, R.J., (1993) *Australian Men and Boys . . . A Picture of Health?* University of Newcastle, and Fletcher, R.J., (1994) *Men's Health.* Australian Community Health Association. Issues paper No. 9, May 1994.

The academic outcomes of boys are discussed in Fletcher, R.J., (1994) *Boys education strategy 1995?* University of Newcastle, and 'Challenges & Opportunities: A Discussion Paper' (1994). A report to the Minister for Education, Training and Youth Affairs on the Inquiry Into Boys' Education, 1994. NSW Government.

The baby-care course is described in Herzig, A.C. and Mali, J.L., *Oh, Boy! Babies!* Boston. Little Brown and Company, 1980.

Cowering behind the bushes

Coosje Griffiths can be contacted by writing to 10a Narla Road, Swanbourne, WA 6010; and by phone and fax on (09) 384 4598.

Resources

Besag, V., (1989) *Bullies and victims in schools.* Open University Press.

Genovese, L., (1992) 'Changing Tracks Program', 21, The Crescent, Helena Valley, WA 6056. Ph: (09) 255 1976.

Griffiths, C., (1993a) 'A system-wide approach to changing attitudes towards the acceptability of bullying or harassment in schools and reducing its prevalence'. In Evans, D., Myhill, M., and Izard, J., (Eds) *Student Behaviour Problems: Positive Initiatives and New Frontiers.* Hawthorn: ACER.

Griffiths, C., (1993b) 'Strategies and resources for turning around a negative class culture'. Unpublished.

Griffiths, C., (1994a) 'Family, School and Community Responses to Bullying in Schools'. Paper given at the National Protective Behaviours Conference, Perth WA, 1994.

Griffiths , C., (1994b) *What Parents Can Do About Bullying.* A booklet to accompany parent workshops.

Griffiths, C., & Martin, M., (1993) 'Student, staff and parent surveys and data collation'. Available from Margaret Martin, 26 Melvista Ave, Claremont, WA, 6010. Ph: (09) 386 4230. Also contact for workshops.

Maines, B., and Robinson, G., (1992) *The No Blame Approach.* England: Lame Duck Publishing.

Martin, M., and Griffiths, C., (1994) 'School Profiles and Data Base on Incidence of Bullying'. Perth: Unpublished.

McGrath, H., and Francey, S., (1992) *Friendly Kids, Friendly Classroom,* Melbourne: Longman Cheshire.

Olweus, D., (1993) *Bullying at School: What We Know and What We Can Do*. Oxford: Blackwell.

Pikas, A., (1989) 'The common concern method for the treatment of mobbing'. In Roland, E., and Munthe, E., (1989) *Bullying: An International Perspective*. London: David Fulton Publishers.

Rigby, K., and Slee, P.T., (1991) 'Bullying among Australian school children: Reported behaviour and attitudes toward victims'. *The Journal of Social Psychology*, 131, 615–627.

Smith, P.K., and Sharp, S., (1994) *School Bullying and How to Cope With It*. London: Routledge.

Page 9 Examples used in this chapter use pseudonyms and combine incidents to protect confidentiality

Page 11 Martin & Griffiths, 1994

Page 12 See Besag, 1989

Page 13 See Pikas, The terms 'shared concern', 'suspected' and 'former' bullies were coined by Pikas.

Page 17 *'Changing Tracks'* is available from L Genovese, 21 The Crescent, Helena Valley WA 6056, Ph: (09) 255 1976

Page 22 Coosje Griffiths, 1994

Page 23 Olweus, 1993

Give me a helmet

For further information on the **student behaviour management strategies** outlined in this chapter contact **Fred Carosi or Ross Tindale** at Canterbury Boys High School, Holden Street, Canterbury, NSW 2193. Telephone (02) 798 8444 or fax (02) 716 7603.

Page 36 The outline of school policies that support the welfare/discipline system.

Year camps and excursions	PD/Health/ PE program	Autonomous Learning Centre	Negotiated rules and procedures
Student-centred learning	Comprehensive documentation	STAR program (Students At Risk)	DEAR scheme (Drop Everything And Read)
Identification of students with special needs	DSC Literacy and Learning Program (Disadvantaged Schools Component)	Antisexism/ antiracism committees and procedures	Peer support program
Vertical classes		**The Glasser System**	Professional development of staff
Remedial programs			Welfare Team and committee
Student representation on school committees (e.g., Finance, School Council, Welfare)	NIM reading program (Neurological Impress Method)	Student Representative	Year camps and excursions
4-period day	Gifted and talented program	Merit award system	Timetabled year group meetings

Breaking the rules

Acknowledgements: My thanks to my editor, Rollo Browne, for his support, gentle persuasion and trust in my work; Peter Clarke whose ideas, inspiration, support and friendship is very much appreciated; and my students without whom this work would not have been possible. **(Kathy Kokori)**

Kathy Kokori can be reached at P O Box 210, Petersham, NSW 2049 or by phone on (02) 525 9629.

Page 46 'Boys Don't Cry', by The Cure, written by Smith, Tolhurst and Dempsey, produced by Parry, June 1979, for Fiction Records, 1986.

Page 47 The poem, 'Masculinity', is available through Kathy Kokori.

The worst class in school?

Allen Littlewood can be contacted by phone on (047) 354 853.

Can I use the word 'gay'?

Maria Pallotta-Chiarolli can be contacted at 17 Cassinya Ave, Ashwood, Victoria 3147 and by phone on (03) 9807 5152.

Acknowledgements: My thanks to colleagues Bill Griffiths (the then principal), Mary Hudson (Director of Studies), Peter Shanahan (the then deputy principal) and Damian Canavan for their support. I also wish to thank the many students who participated enthusiastically and sincerely in my classes, and to students and teachers from other schools in Australia who have taken the time to write and chat with me. And, of course, as always, to Jon, who has never stopped teaching. **(Maria Pallotta-Chiarolli)**

Page 67 Introducing homophobia Although using the standard definitions of homophobia (such as fear of same-sex affection and homosexuality) it was also important to include the colloquial meanings of the term, as the students interpreted it as being anti-gay.

Page 68 Teaching specific units Much of the later work undertaken on homophobia was part of a whole-school gender and equity project funded by the Catholic Education Office. Reports and articles on the project may be found in Pallotta-Chiarolli, Maria (1990), 'The Female Stranger in a Boys School', *Gender And Education* Vol. 2, No.2, United Kingdom; Pallotta-Chiarolli, Maria (1992), 'Gender Issues and the Education of Boys', *Catholic Ethos* No. 7, National Catholic Education Commission; *The Gen* (Gender and Equity Network Newsletter) DEET Publication, March 1994; Pallotta-Chiarolli, Maria (1994), 'Educating the Person: Gender and Equity Issues in Catholic Schools' and 'Educating the Person: Implementing Gender and Equity Action in Catholic Schools' in *Conference:* Journal of Catholic Education Conference, Vol. 11, No.2 and Vol. 11, No. 3, Victorian Catholic Education Office; Pallotta-Chiarolli, Maria (1994), 'Butch Minds the Baby: Boys Minding Masculinity in the English Classroom', *Interpretations:* Journal of the Western Australian English Teachers Association, Vol. 27, No.2.

The school had also been personally touched by issues of homosexuality and AIDS with the death of a highly-respected and much-loved teacher and colleague. The experiences were publicised through the publishing of my book *Someone You Know: A Friend's Farewell,* (1991) Adelaide: Wakefield Press. (Royalties are donated to the Bobby Goldsmith Foundation for People Living with AIDS.)

Page 68 'Antihomophobic principles and objectives will inform what we teach . . .' Several texts are now available which provide philosophical and theoretical as well as practical discussions on antihomophobia and pedagogy. I recommend the following: Harbeck, Karen M., (ed) (1992), *Coming Out of the Classroom Closet,* New York: Harrington Park Press; Epstein, D., (ed), *Challenging Lesbian and Gay Inequalities In Education,* Buckingham: Open University Press; Rench, J., (1990), *Understanding Sexual Identity: A Book For Gay Teens and Their Friends,* New York: Lerner.

Page 69 Research into the whole-school approach Epstein, D., (ed), *Challenging Lesbian and Gay Inequalities in the Classroom, (ibid).*

Page 70 'Most of my antihomophobic work with boys was done in the English classroom' For the purposes of this article I am not able to elaborate on my work and the work of colleagues and other teachers around Australia in English. However content, strategies and resources have been documented in my publications: Pallotta-Chiarolli, Maria, (1994), 'A Terrain of Intervention and Resistance: AIDS and Sexuality Issues in the English Classroom', *Realising the Future,* Australian Association of the Teachers of English National Conference Papers, Perth, July; Pallotta-Chiarolli, Maria, (1994), 'Connecting Landscapes of Marginality: AIDS and Sexuality Issues in the English Classroom' in Parsons, W. , and Goodwin, R., (eds) *Landscape And Identity: Perspectives From Australia,* Adelaide: University of South Australia Centre for Childrens Literature and Auslib Press.

Texts that will guide teachers and parents in locating ***appropriate antihomopho-bic texts for English studies*** are: Clyde, Laurel A., and Lobban, Marjorie, (1992), *Out of the Closet and Into the Classroom,* Port Melbourne, Victoria, ALIA Thorpe; Pallotta-Chiarolli, Maria (1994), 'Butch Minds The Baby: Boys Minding Masculinity in the English Classroom', *op.cit.* A useful theoretical reference is Harris, Simon, (1990), *Lesbian and Gay Issues In the English Classroom,* Philadelphia, Open University Press.

Page 70 ***'Texts on Australian gay, lesbian and bisexual history . . .'*** Recommended texts which include much useful material for Australian Studies and Australian History are Aldrich, Robert, and Wotherspoon, Garry, (eds) (1992), *Gay Perspectives: Essays In Australian Gay Culture,* University of Sydney, University of Sydney Press; Aldrich, Robert, (ed) (1993), *Gay Perspectives II: More Essays In Australian Gay Culture,* Australian Centre for Gay and Lesbian Research, University of Sydney Press; French, Robert, (1993), *Camping by a Billabong: Gay and Lesbian Stories From Australian History,* Sydney, BlackWattle Press; Hodge, Dino, (1993), *Did You Meet Any Malagas? A Homosexual History of Australia's Tropical Capital,* Darwin, Little Gem Publications. Unfortunately, there is still a lack of material on lesbian history in Australia.

Page 71 ***'A short story on the experiences of a gay Jewish man'*** Sharp, Cameron, (1994), 'Nehmi' in Carr, A., (ed) *Outrage 1995 Gay and Lesbian Short Story Anthology,* Melbourne, Designer Publications.

Page 71 ***Concepts of 'normal' and 'abnormal' from other societies*** New Internationalist Cooperative (ed) (1989), 'Pride and Prejudice: Homosexuality', *New Internationalist* No. 201, November issue provides extremely useful international and historical information as well as questionnaires that encourage student discussion.

Page 71 ***Access to antihomophobic texts*** Feminist bookshops and gay bookshops (such as Murphy Sisters and Imprints in Adelaide, Hares and Hyenas, and Shrew Feminist Bookshop in Melbourne, and the Feminist Bookshop and the Bookshop Darlinghurst in Sydney) as well as specialist libraries such as the Darling House Community Library (part of the South Australian AIDS Council) and the Womens Studies Resource Centre in Adelaide are great sources for teachers and students. *XY: Men, Sex, Politics* is a very useful journal of articles, poetry and stories that are antihomophobic as well as antiracist and profeminist. Kits such as *Block Out: Fighting Homophobia* (Mahamati and Miller, Kenton Penley (1994), Adelaide, Second Story Youth Health Centre are available. GALTAS (Gay and Lesbian Teachers and Students Association) based in Sydney and PARENT-FLAG (Parents and Friends for Lesbians and Gays) can provide much material and advice as well as speakers and workshop facilitators. Membership is open to all sexualities.

Page 73 ***'One school in London'*** Patrick, Paul and Sanders, Susan A.L., (1994), 'Lesbian and Gay Issues in the Classroom in Epstein,D., (ed) *Challenging Lesbian and Gay Inequalities In the Classroom, op.cit,* p. 119.

Page 74 ***'This kind of response can be very detrimental and hurtful'*** Rogers, Marigold, (1994), 'Growing Up Lesbian: The Role of the School' in Epstein, D., (ed) *Challenging Lesbian and Gay Inequalities In Education, op.cit,* p. 39.

Page 76 ***Integrating antihomophobic concepts into broader themes (social justice, preju-dice, discrimination)*** Here are two examples from letters received from students in schools throughout Australia whose teachers encouraged this 'connecting marginalities' approach in studying my book *Someone You Know* :

'I can now relate the prejudice that Anne Frank was subjected to for being Jewish, the prejudice Steve Biko felt from the white South Africans in *Cry Freedom,* to how

Jon felt about his disease and his sexuality. He, like Anne Frank and Steve Biko, was faced with society's negative views about differences.'

'I am now more aware of what is happening around me. I don't regard homosexuality as a disease anymore or a disorder. I just see it as a characteristic of a person, like black skin or being Vietnamese.'

Page 76 Antihomophobia work as part of the overall development of the student We can encourage students to empathise with the fears and questions inherent in coming out as gay or lesbian by asking them to reflect on their own experiences of being discriminated against – boys resisting limiting gender stereotypes, students of non-English-speaking and Aboriginal backgrounds can discuss their own forms of marginality and connect with gay marginality. For material linking ethnicity and homosexuality, see Pallotta-Chiarolli, Maria, (1992), 'What About Me? Lesbians of Italian Background' in Herne, K., Travaglia, J., and Weiss, E., (eds) *Who Do You Think You Are? Second Generation Immigrant Women In Australia.* Sydney, Womens Redress Press; Pallotta-Chiarolli, Maria, (1994), 'Roses' in P. Moss (ed) *Voicing the Difference,* Adelaide, Wakefield Press; Pallotta-Chiarolli, Maria, (1991), *Someone You Know, op.cit.;* Pallotta-Chiarolli, Maria (1994), 'Its Not My Death I'm Worried About', *AIDS Awareness Week Bulletin* December, No.2, Australian Federation of AIDS Organisations. At the time of writing this chapter, two articles were in the process of being published: 'Only Your Labels Split Me' – Interweaving Ethnicity and Sexuality Studies' in *English in Australia,* August, 1995; and "Mestizaje": Interweaving Cultural Multiplicity and Gender Codes in English Studies' in *Interpretations: Journal of the Western Australian English Teachers Association,* forthcoming August, 1995.

The experiences of lesbians and bisexual women need to be presented as part of a **gender inclusive curriculum.** An excellent novel that deals with lesbian students and lesbian teachers within a homophobic school environment is *Annie on My Mind* by Nancy Garden (1982), Canada, HarperCollins. A recent novel is Catherine Johns (1994), *Me Mum's a Queer,* Stirling, South Australia, Epona Press. The links between racism, sexism and homophobia are clearly drawn through the characters from diverse cultural backgrounds. The text has a few flaws in its one-sided view of sexism in ethnic families and bisexuality as a 'cop-out', providing material for critical discussion in class debate. In relation to HIV-positive lesbians, excerpts from the autobiography by Fran Peavey (1990) *A Shallow Pool of Time: An HIV+ Woman Grapples With the AIDS Epidemic,* Philadelphia, New Society Publishers, are very useful.

Page 78 'You're going against the Church' I cannot enter into a detailed discussion here of homophobia in schools and Church teaching, although further information is available from me.

Page 78 Catholic schools addressing homophobia Catholic Education Offices are gradually beginning to prepare materials challenging homophobia. The most progressive is the *Human Sexuality* kit from the South Australian Catholic Education Office prepared by a team of teachers coordinated by Geraldine Rice. The Catholic Education Office of the Parramatta Diocese in New South Wales has appointed a part-time teacher/consultant, Dominic Hearne, to conduct workshops on HIV/AIDS and homophobia. The Human Rights Foundation (1984), *Demystifying Homosexuality,* New York, Irvington Publishers, provides practical exercises and lesson plans that are extremely useful for Religious Education and Social Studies lessons. Other useful materials that explore Catholic church/school and homophobia issues are: Shinnick, Maurice Fr., (1991), 'Homosexuality', *SA Catholic,* September: 5, South Australian Catholic Church Office; Keenan, Tony, (1993), 'AIDS Education and Catholic Schools', *Independent Education,* Victoria, June: 9–12; Pallotta-Chiarolli, Maria, (1994), 'Inscribing AIDS and Sexuality: Who Has the Right To Write? Who Listens?' in *Australian Multicultural Book Review* 2(2); Pallotta-Chiarolli, Maria, (1994), 'The "Real Voyage of Discovery": Auto/Biography, Reflexivity and Spiritual Journeying' in Griffiths, M., and Keating, R., (eds) *Religion, Literature and the Arts,* Sydney, Australian Catholic University.

Each Church has its own gay and lesbian groups in the capital cities such as UNITY in the Uniting Church and ACCEPTANCE in the Catholic Church. These groups may provide valuable resources as well as possible guest-speakers. The

Brisbane Acceptance Group, in conjunction with the Archbishop, has developed a resource and teaching kit for use in parishes and schools.

Video resource See *Mates*, a 23-minute VHS video on HIV/AIDS-related discrimination in a school setting. Winner of the 1993 Gold Mobie Award. Produced by Health Media for the New South Wales Department of School Education (1993). Funded by the AIDS Bureau, NSW Health Department.

Working with boys and masculinity

Rollo Browne can be contacted at P O Box 1042, Rozelle, NSW 2039 and by phone on (02) 555 8424.

Page 84 Levels of resistance framework This framework is drawn from what is sometimes called the 'discount hierarchy' or the 'discomfort cycle'. This sets out the various ways in which people dismiss or discount a problem so they don't have to come to terms with it. The discount hierarchy was developed by Peg Flandau-West and was first used in the education and training of Child Sexual Assault workers. See reference in *Mandatory Notification of Child Sexual Assault – A Training Package for Health Workers*, Sexual Assault Education Unit, Sydney, NSW Department of Health (1987).

Page 88 Evaluation The levels of resistance framework can be used as an evaluation tool. One way is to create a questionnaire in relation to hassling and harassing others by writing a number of questions for each position (see Fig 1). Each boy completes the questionnaire and his scores are averaged to give his position. To match the positions on the continuum, the lowest score is *1 – Denial*, the highest is *5 – Action*. Scores for the whole class give a cumulative picture of how widely the class as a whole are spread, or if there is a distinct split or subgroups. One danger in evaluating attitudes by questionnaires is that some boys may tell you what they think you want to hear. Some groups might even appear to go backwards after the initial assessment as they get more honest about how they really think and behave. Ideally the questionnaire would be backed up by playground and classroom observation.

Figure 1 Issues in masculinity
Questionnaire 2: Violence, Harassment and Hassling in the Playground

When we hear about violence and harassment in schools, boys' behaviour is mentioned in the same breath. Boys are seen as macho, aggressive and causing trouble in school playgrounds. This questionnaire is anonymous and looks at what we feel about the issue. At the end of each question, respondents are asked to delete either 'Agree' or 'Disagree'.

1. When boys put other boys down it affects me. I'm sick of it and I'd like to know what we can do.
2. If I see boys giving others a hard time I join in.
3. I don't want to harass and hassle others in front of my mates but I don't know what else to do.
4. Boys' behaviour is a problem. Someone should do something about it.
5. Most of the time hassling other guys is funny.
6. I look up to guys who get their way by using strong-arm tactics.
7. I'd feel OK speaking out honestly against verbal abuse and harassment.
8. I avoid saying anything about it because I don't want to be picked on.
9. Everybody hassles – so who cares? It really doesn't matter if some people get upset.
10. Boys harass each other, so it's OK.
11. I think guys should take the lead in doing something about this issue.
12. The ones who get picked on, ask for it. It's their problem.
13. I'd be interested in working on this issue with other groups.
14. I hassle others in front of my mates because I can't stop. At least it gets something going.
15. I want to do something – but how will my friends react if I speak up?
16. It makes me feel bad – but what can I do?

17. I switch off or get annoyed when people start talking about sexism and boys' aggression and violence.
18. I'd like to give more thought to the way I behave, as long as I keep my friends.
19. I know I have some responsibility for what goes on in the playground but I don't want to draw attention to myself.
20. I wouldn't choose to do a course on masculinity and male issues.

Boys and relationships

David Shores can be contacted at Boys and Relationships, 2 Dew Street, Kent Town, South Australia, 5067 and by phone on (08) 362 7511. A package comprising the *Boys and Relationships Program Manual* and edited transcripts of the training session is available at the above address. Please send a cheque or money order for $49.90 (which includes postage and handling within Australia).

Looking to fathers

Richard Fletcher can be reached at the Faculty of Medicine and Health Sciences, University of Newcastle, NSW 2308 and by phone on (049) 216 401.

Page 117 A parent and teacher survey designed to raise awareness of boys issues has been developed by the Men's Health Project, University of Newcastle (see below).

Page 118 An inspiring book describing fathers from poor suburbs in the USA getting involved in preschools is Levine J.A., Murphy D.T., Wilson S., *Getting Men Involved*, New York, Scholastic Inc., 1993.

Page 119 The NSW government inquiry Challenges & Opportunities: A Discussion Paper (1994) – a report to the Minister for Education, Training and Youth Affairs on the Inquiry Into Boys' Education 1994. NSW Government.

Parent–Teacher Survey

Respondents were asked to tick one box in both 'A' and 'B' groups. These followed each question.

A. Your reaction
I knew this.   ☐
I've wondered about this.   ☐
I am very surprised to hear this.   ☐

B. Your concern
I am not concerned about this.   ☐
I am a little concerned about this.   ☐
I am very concerned about this.   ☐

OUTCOMES FOR BOYS – ACADEMIC
1. 10% fewer boys than girls complete Year 12.
2. 75% of school suspensions are boys.
3. 60% of school counsellor referrals are boys.
4. Nine times as many boys as girls are in special classes for emotional and behavioural disturbance.
5. Three times as many boys as girls are in language or intensive reading classes.
6. Boys do considerably worse in Basic Skills English tests at all ages.

OUTCOMES FOR BOYS – LIFE
7. Boys die at twice the rate for girls from injuries.
8. Juvenile males are nine times more likely than girls to commit serious assaults.
9. Young males suicide at five times the rate for girls.
10. Boys are nine times more likely than girls to be convicted on a drugs charge.
11. Young men are six times more likely than young women to be killed at work, and seven times more likely to be permanently disabled.
12. 97% of those who are HIV positive are males; 98% of deaths from AIDS are male.
13. On any one day in Australia there are 1100 boys and 200 girls in custody.
14. 100% of reported rapes are by males.

The sources for the figures used in the survey are as follows:

Question 1 Johnston, S., *Retention Rates: More Than Just Counting Heads*, Department of Education, Queensland, 1990.

Questions 2, 4 and 5 Hunter Region figures for 1991. McMahon, J., 'Sex Imbalance in Students with Educational Needs'. Unpublished paper. (At the time of writing the author was a Cluster Director in NSW Department of School Education.)

Question 3 NSW Department of Education, 'School Counselling Service Program Evaluation', 1989. Unpublished report.

Question 6 Australian Council for Educational Research *Basic Skills Testing Program Public Report 1991.*

Question 7 Australian Bureau of Statistics, *1992, Causes of Death Australia Cat. No. 3303.0*

Questions 8 and 13 Mukhurjee, Satyanshu K., *The Size of the Crime Problem In Australia*, Australian Institute of Criminology, 1990.

Question 9 Harrison, J., Moller, J., Dolinis, J., *Australian Injury Prevention Bulletin*, National Injury Surveillance Unit. 5, February 1994.

Question 11 Fletcher, R,J., (1993) *Australian Men and Boys . . . A Picture of Health?*, University of Newcastle.

Question 12 *Australian HIV Surveillance Report*, January 1993, Vol.9, No.1.

A number of these sources are applicable to the Hunter region or NSW in particular. Although other local or regional figures may vary, the general picture of males having poor academic and social outcomes seems to hold across Australia.

It's not the way guys think!

Wayne Martino can be contacted at Unit 2, 6 Salvado Street, Cottesloe, WA 6011 and by phone on (09) 385 3439.

Page 126 Boys' attitudes to studying English The following researchers have documented the link between masculinity and learning within the subject of English:

Curtis, M., (1992),'The Performance of Girls and Boys in Subject English', *Interpretations*, Vol. 25, No. 1.

Kenway, J.,(1987), 'Is Gender an Issue in English Teaching?' *Interpretations*, Vol. 20, No. 1.

Lee, A., (1980), 'Together We Learn to Read and Write: Sexism and Literacy', in Spender, D., (ed) *Learning to Lose: Sexism and Education*, London, The Womens Press.

Martino, W., (1993), 'Boys Underachievement and Under-representation in Subject English', thesis submitted in partial fulfilment for the Degree of Master of Education (Honours), School of Education, Murdoch University.

Martino, W., (1995), 'Gendered Learning Practices: Exploring the Costs of Hegemonic Masculinity for Girls and Boys in Schools', paper presented at the Gender Equity Taskforce Conference, Canberra.

Page 126 Boys and girls in class For further reading about the differences between boys and girls' gendered practices in schools see the following:

Clarricoates, K., (1980). 'The Importance of Being Ernest . . . Emma . . . Tom . . . Jane: the Perception and Categorisation of Gender Conformity and Gender Deviation in Primary Schools', in Deem, R., (ed) *Schooling for Women's Work*, London:, Routledge & Kegan Paul.

Davies, B., (1989), 'The Discursive Production of the Male–Female Dualism in School Settings', *Oxford Review of Education*, Vol. 15. No. 3.

Deem, R., (1984), *Co-education Reconsidered*, Milton Keynes & Philadelphia, Open University Press.

Mahony, P., (1985), *Schools for Boys? Co-education Re-assessed*, London, Hutchinson.

Stanworth, M., (1983), *Gender and Schooling*, London, Hutchinson.

Page 127 Survey: students' perceptions of English The research included in this section is based on my M.Ed. (Hons) thesis, School of Education, Murdoch University.

Page 127 'The hard part – expressing feelings' For further discussion about this denial of expressing emotion which appears to be at the basis of dominant models of masculinity see:

Forsey, C., (1990), *The Making of Men*, Footscray, West Education Centre.
Hite, S., (1980), *The Hite Report on Male Sexuality*, New York:, Alfred A. Knopf Inc.
Mac an Ghaill, M., (1994), *The Making of Men*, Buckingham, Open University Press.
McGill, M., (1985), *The McGill Report on Male Intimacy*, New York, Holt, Rhinehart & Winston.

Page 127 The influences of sport For further reading about the influences of sport in the formation and construction of hegemonic masculinities see the following:

Klein, M., (1990), 'The Macho World of Sport - A Forgotten Realm? Some Introductory Remarks', *International Review for the Sociology of Sport*, Vol. 25. No. 3.
Martino, W., (1994), 'The Gender Bind and Subject English: Exploring Questions of Masculinity in Developing Interventionist Strategies in the English Classroom', *English in Australia*, No. 107, March.
Messner, M., (1990), 'Boyhood, Organised Sports, and the Construction of Masculinities', *Journal of Contemporary Ethnography*, Vol. 18. No. 4.
Messner, M., & Sabo, D., (199), *Sport, Men and the Gender Order: Critical Feminist Perspectives*, Champaign, Illinois, Human Kinetics Books.

Page 129 The different values boys and girls attach to Maths, Science and English For further discussion about the gendered construction of the curriculum, with a particular focus on Maths and Science, see:

Kelly, A., (ed) (1987), *Science for Girls?* Milton Keynes and Philadelphia, Open University Press.
Weinreich-Haste, H., (1986), 'Brother Sun, Sister Moon: Does Rationality Overcome Dualistic World View?', in Harding, J., (ed) *Perspectives on Gender and Science*, London, The Falmer Press.

Page 130 Homophobia and masculinity For a further discussion of the role of homophobia in the policing of masculinity in schools see:

Connell, R., (1989), 'Cool Guys, Swots and Wimps: The Interplay of Masculinity and Education', *Oxford Review of Education*, Vol. 15. No. 3.
Kessler, S., Ashenden, D.J., Connell, R.W., and Dowsett, G.W. ,(1985), 'Gender Relations in Secondary Schooling', *Sociology of Education*, Vol. 58: 34–48.
Mac an Ghaill, M., (1994), *The Making of Men*, Buckingham, Open University Press.
Wolpe, A., (1988), *Within School Walls*, London and New York, Routledge.

Page 130 Craig's story This is not the student's real name; it has been changed for obvious reasons.

Page 132 'The Altar of the Family' by Michael Wilding This short story is included in a textbook, entitled *Gendered Fictions* (published by Chalkface Press, 1995), which I have written with Bronwyn Mellor. In this book we have chosen texts and set up activities around them to direct students' attention to the construction of gender and its effects. The focus is on the construction of masculinity, and through text-based activities we attempt to engage students in an examination of the effects of dominant models of masculinity in a non threatening way. In other words, we use fiction and nonfiction texts to target masculinity for specific analysis in the English classroom. For a more detailed and theoretical discussion of the ways in which a group of boys responded to this particular text, see:

Martino, W., (1995), 'Deconstructing Masculinity in the English Classroom: A Site for Reconstituting Gendered Subjectivity', *Gender and Education*, Vol. 7. No. 2 ,UK.

Page 134 The father See Martino and Mellor (1995), *Gendered Fictions*, Chalkface Press, page 62.
Page 134 The son *ibid.*

Young and powerful

Maureen Moran can be contacted at Young and Powerful, 62 Leycester Street, Lismore, NSW 2480 and by phone on (066) 217 719.

Being 'cool' and a reader

Gwenda Sanderson can be contacted at Arrendell Primary Education Centre, 5 Merinda Close, Adamstown Heights, NSW 2289 and by phone on (049) 42 3000.

Listed below are books that the boys at my centre enjoy (presented from the easier to the more difficult books).

For boys commencing reading look for picture books with fast action, repetitive words and lots of fun in them: *Little Rabbit Foo Foo* (Walker); Robert Munsch books, such as *Good Families Don't* and *David's Father* and *Pigs* (Annick) are very popular; as are all Babette Cole titles, e.g., *Hurrah for Ethelyn* and *Supermoo* and *Three Cheers for Errol* (Mammoth).

'Bridging books' – the books between picture books and novels:

Look for titles in the *Jets* series, e.g., *Almost Goodbye Guzzler* (Collins), the *Skinny* books series, e.g., *Foxer Gets Smart* (Collins), and the *Dipper* series, e.g., *Pink Fluffy Slippers* (Omnibus).

'Pre-novel' – other special popular titles for readers who are not quite ready for full novel are:

Winter, Tim, *The Bugalugs Bum Thief* (Puffin);
Scieszka, Jon, *The Frog Prince Continued, The Stinky Cheeseman and Other Fairly Stupid Tales, The True Story of the Three Little Pigs* and the *Time Warp Trio* series, (Puffin);
Dahl, Roald, *Magic Finger, Fantastic Mr Fox, Georges Marvellous Medicine, The Twits, The Minpins* and *The Giraffe, the Pelly and Me* (Puffin);
Jennings, Paul, all titles, including *Gismo, The Paw Thing* and *The Cabbage Patch Fib.*

The following are books of *novel length*, that the boys enjoy because of humour, risqué parts or horror – or just because they are a 'good read':

Ball, Duncan, all *Selby* titles (Collins);
Clark, Margaret, *Tina Tuff, Plastic City, Fat Chance* and *Weird Warren* (Omnibus);
Dann, Max, *Clark* (Puffin);
Fine, Anne , *Bills New Frock, Madame Doubtfire* and other titles (Puffin);
Heasley, Murray, *Shuz* (Omnibus);
Harris, Christine, *Outer Face* and *Buried Secrets* (Random);
Gleitzman, Morris, all titles, *Blabbermouth, Stickybeak* and *Two Weeks With the Queen* (Pan);
Oswald, Debra, *The Return of the Baked Bean* (Puffin);
Mattingley, Christobel, *No Gun for Asmir* (Puffin);
Fleischman, Sid, *The Whipping Boy* (Mammoth);
Simons, Moya, *Dead Meat* (Omnibus);
Stine, R. L., *Goosebumps,* the *Fear Street* series and other titles (Scholastic);
Stephens, Michael, *The Ghost Train, Eddy the Great, The Prince of Kelvin Mall* and *Titans* (Allen & Unwin);
Spinelli, Jerry, *Maniac McGee* (Scholastic);
Wilson, David Henry, *There's a Wolf in My Pudding* and other titles (Pan);
Winton, Tim, *Lockie Leonard Human Scumbuster* and *Lockie Leonard Human Torpedo* (Pan);
Jacques, Brian, *The Redwall Trilogy, Mariel, Salamandastron* and other titles (Random).

Look out for:
- books based on current films, e.g., Strasser, Todd, *Free Willy* (Puffin);
- humorous poetry, e.g., Macleod, Doug, *Sister Madge's Book of Nuns* (Omnibus);
- joke books; books with tapes, e.g., Disney's *Read with Me* series, *Jets* book and tape sets, ABC children's book tapes.

Other authors to look out for are: Jeremy Strong, Jacqueline Wilson and Geoffrey McSkimming.

I'll get you at lunch!

Peter Clarke can be contacted at P O Box 1481, Potts Point, NSW 2011 and by phone on (02) 368 0108.

Page 172 'Parents and guardians were asked to reveal specific behaviours that their sons had displayed in the previous six months Achenbach, T. M., *Manual for Child Behaviour Checklist/* 4–18 and 1991 Profile, Burlington, VT, University of Vermont, Department of Psychiatry, 1991.

Page 174 Using a kit of black-and-white photos Catholic Education Office, Photo-language Kit (Human Values A & B), Sydney, 1993.

Page 174 'Maintaining interest' Hunt, G., Koszegi, B., and Shores, D., *Boys and Relationships: A Program for Pre-Adolescent Boys*, Tea Tree Gully, Education Department of South Australia, 1993.

Power and classroom relations

Rollo Browne can be contacted at P O Box 1042, Rozelle, NSW 2039 and by phone on (02) 555 8424.

Boys' team also does well

Su Langker can be contacted at 26 Duxford Street, Paddington, NSW 2021 and by phone on (02) 380 5563.

Changing the lives of boys

Richard Fletcher can be reached at the Faculty of Medicine and Health Sciences, University of Newcastle, NSW 2308 and by phone on (049) 216 401.

Nurturing boys, developing skills

Peter Ireland can be contacted at MacKillop Senior College, P O Box 1201, Port Macquarie, NSW 2444 and by phone on (065) 83 4611.

Page 221 April Fool's Day by Bryce Courtenay (published by Reed Books Australia) Peter Ireland and Finch Publishing are most appreciative of the kind permission of Reed Books Australia to reproduce two passages from this work.

Schools and the construction of masculinity

Rollo Browne can be contacted at P O Box 1042, Rozelle, NSW 2039 and by phone on (02) 555 8424.

Social construction of gender The best description we have of why males and females behave the way they do is known as the 'social construction of gender'. This theory was developed by R. W. Connell, D. J. Ashenden, S. Kessler and G. Dowsett after extensive interviews with students into the ways they explained their behaviour, in particular the way they decided what behaviour they used at any given moment. The most accessible version of the social construction of gender I have found is Colin Hocking's chapter, 'Framework and Foothold' in the video kit, *Boys Will Be Boys*, Open Channel, Victoria, 1986. See also Kessler et al (1985), 'Gender Relations In Secondary Schooling', *Sociology of Education*, 58: pp 34–48.

Key areas where schools are implicated In terms of having an impact on the areas where schools are involved in the construction of gender, there is substantial agreement among the major educational sociologists in Australia. The areas include: peer group interaction and pupil culture; play; student–teacher relations; control and discipline; and curriculum, knowledge and assessment.

The challenge is to examine how schools can challenge the gender regime in each of these areas. See Bob Connell (1994) 'Knowing About Masculinity, Teaching Boys And Men', paper for Pacific Sociological Association Conference, San Diego, April 1994, and Jane Kenway (1994) Submission on behalf of Women in Education, NSW cited in *Draft Report On The Inquiry Into Boys' Education 1994*, NSW Government Advisory Committee On Education, Training And Tourism.

The gender regime To get a sense of the gender regime in your school consider the following aspects of school life: (You may think of other relevant areas.)

- how power is modelled and exerted among staff;
- who enforces the school rules and how;
- how teachers control and discipline students;
- the language used by teachers (e.g., to describe subjects, to discipline students, to refer to minority and other groups, etc);
- the kind of subjects the school offers; how students are encouraged by various male and female teachers to, for example, play sport, enter debates and choose subjects;
- the way the content is structured in the curriculum and the activities used in the classroom;
- the way success and failure is treated, and how it is assessed;
- the way assemblies are structured – who gets the lion's share of attention at assemblies;
- what awards are given and how status is accorded to students by the school;
- what is rewarded by peers, and by the opposite sex;
- the policies behind the school welfare system– how it really operates and who does it.

Aggression Replacement Training programs These involve three components: skill streaming (social skills, dealing with feelings, alternatives to aggression, dealing with stress, planning skills), anger-control training and moral reasoning.

Skill streaming programs were developed in the US in the 1980s – see Goldstein, A., et al (1980), *Skill-streaming the adolescent* and McGinnis, E., and Goldstein, A., (1984) *Skill-streaming the Elementary School Child: A Guide For Teaching Prosocial Skills.* The full program is contained in *The Prepare Curriculum: Teaching Prosocial Competencies* again by Goldstein *et al* (1988).

The program draws heavily on small-group activities and includes some role play. All titles are published by Research Press, Illinois, and are available from Astam Books, 57–61 John Street, Leichhardt, NSW 2040, phone (02) 566 4400 and fax (02) 566 4411.

Research on the program's effectiveness is presented in a paper from the Conference of Australian Guidance and Counsellors Association in Sydney, 'Goldstein, A., and Glick, B., (1993) "Aggression Replacement Training: Curriculum and Evaluation"'.